D1230569

A GALLA MONARCHY

Jimma Abba Jifar, Ethiopia

1830–1932

A Galla Monarchy

Jimma Abba Jifar, Ethiopia
1830–1932

HERBERT S. LEWIS

The University of Wisconsin Press
Madison and Milwaukee, 1965

Published by the University of Wisconsin Press
Madison and Milwaukee
P.O. Box 1379, Madison, Wisconsin 53701

Printed in the United States of America by the George Banta Company, Inc., Menasha, Wisconsin

Library of Congress Catalog Card Number 65–24185

To my parents and my wife

Acknowledgments

I wish to express my indebtedness to some of the people who have contributed to this book. Foremost among my debts are those to Professors Conrad M. Arensberg, Morton H. Fried, and Joseph H. Greenberg, who were teachers and guides throughout my graduate study, and who read and criticized successive drafts of this work. I also want to thank Professor Morton Klass, who read the work and offered valuable advice, and Professor Wolf Leslau, who first introduced me to the study of Ethiopia and its peoples. The work was supported by a fellowship from the Ford Foundation, and I wish to express my gratitude to that organization. I am indebted to the University of Wisconsin Cartographic Laboratory for preparing the maps which appear in this book. My wife, Marcia, has given me constant aid and encouragement throughout the years of graduate study, and during the preparation of this book.

To His Imperial Majesty Haile Selassie I and the officials of the Imperial Ethiopian Government who permitted my wife and me to live and carry on research in Jimma and elsewhere in Ethiopia, and to the many friends in Addis Ababa and Jimma who made our life there exciting and rewarding, we owe a debt of gratitude that it is a pleasure to acknowledge. It is, of course, to the people of Jiren and Jimma Abba Jifar that we are most indebted. They took us into their homes, let us live in their community, and freely shared with us their knowledge of the kingdom of Jimma Abba Jifar. We could not have asked for kinder hosts.

H. S. L.

Madison, Wisconsin
July, 1964

Contents

Introduction

The Empire of Ethiopia, as it exists today, is an amalgamation of the ancient kingdom of Abyssinia with a host of other ethnic groups, tribes, and kingdoms. One hundred and fifty years ago the Abyssinians occupied most of the land north of present-day Addis Ababa, but the territory to the south, from the Sudan to the Somalilands, was independent. This large area included scores of distinct peoples, some organized into kingdoms, others living in simpler and smaller socio-political units. It was not until the 1800's that the Amhara, under vigorous leadership and armed with modern rifles, managed to subdue and occupy the southern regions. While a great deal is known of the history of the northern area during the past two thousand years, much less is known of the history of the southern peoples.

Among the ethnic groups of southern Ethiopia the largest is the Galla. The Galla first appeared in Ethiopian history in the sixteenth century when in a series of migrations and conquests they occupied much of the land of southern Ethiopia. There has been much romantic speculation about them—their culture, personality, origins, migrations, and their impact on other African societies. According to the traditional view, the Galla were a society of democratic, egalitarian, age-graded pastoral nomads. In this book I shall present a picture of one Galla group which radically departs from this view.

The Galla kingdom of Jimma Abba Jifar (1830–1932), far from being democratic and egalitarian, was a remarkably centralized, well-organized, and powerful monarchy. In addition to presenting a description of the kingdom, this book will seek to trace its origins and development and to suggest how a people with very different traditions could have produced such a political system. Because the Galla are generally represented as a people "to whom . . . the concentration of power in the hands of one man was repugnant,"[1] the Galla monarchies (of which there were seven or more) have generally been explained as borrowings from the monarchically organized non-Galla peoples with whom they came into contact, or else as the result of the conquest of such peoples. One argument of the book is that the kingdom of Jimma Abba Jifar was peculiarly Galla in many respects and that its formation was due less to borrowing and conquest than to cultural and political processes within nineteenth-century Galla, and western Ethiopian, society. The socio-political organization and milieu of the non-monarchical Galla which formed the background of these states is considered in Chapter II, along with the history of Jimma Abba Jifar itself. I shall also try to demonstrate, throughout the book, important differences between Jimma

1 Huntingford, 1955: 55.

Abba Jifar and the non-Galla monarchies which it knew and from which it borrowed many items.

In another, more general, sense this book is meant to be a contribution to the growing field of political anthropology and the study of African political systems. To a great extent the study of politics involves the study of leadership and power, and this work focuses briefly on the transformation of leadership into power and then on the successful exercise of monarchical power in one African state. Much of the emphasis is on the processes of government, the functions and tasks of officials, the powers of the king, and the elements which contributed to the maintenance of central control by the king. Whereas many writers have concentrated on those African kingdoms in which the central authority was weak and the state was constantly shifting its borders and structure, I have concentrated on a kingdom where no such looseness existed and have tried to show why it did not. As a presentation and analysis of a strongly centralized and unified state this book complements the studies of "segmentary states" by A. Southall, L. A. Fallers, and J. A. Barnes.

I have not always emphasized the same types of data that other writers have. For example, I have given far less weight to descriptions of kinship, lineage systems, and local social structure, and emphasized, to a greater extent than is usual, the operations of the government and its officers, the organization of activities, and the power and prerogatives of the king. The shift in emphasis is due in part to the nature of the society and polity itself, and in part to my concern with the problem of the maintenance of power.

This study is based primarily upon field work carried out in Ethiopia from December, 1958, to April, 1960. About eleven months of that time were spent in the area of the old kingdom of Jimma Abba Jifar in southwestern Ethiopia. The monarchy under study came to an end in 1932 when the Ethiopian government began to administer the area directly from Addis Ababa; it is now one district (*awraja*) in the province of Kafa. The province also includes about six other formerly autonomous kingdoms, among them Kafa, which I shall be comparing to Jimma. Although the name "Jimma" in this book is used for the whole kingdom, there is now a modern town called Jimma. It is located on the site of Jimma Abba Jifar's greatest market, Hirmata, and is about two hundred miles—by road—west-southwest of Addis Ababa. The town of Jimma served the Italians and now serves the Ethiopian government as the provincial capital. The old capital of the kingdom is at Jiren, several miles from the new town. The grandsons of the last king still live there, but the palace is rapidly falling into ruin, as the administration has shifted to the governor's office in Jimma town. The governor is an appointee of the emperor and is generally an Amhara. Most of the governor's aids and regional administrators are also Amhara, although the sub-sub-sub-governors (*abba k'oro*) and a few sub-sub-governors (*warada gĕži*) are Galla and represent noble Jimma families.

Although the monarchical organization described in the following pages no longer operates, local community structure remains basically unchanged. There has been no trend toward wage labor, labor migration, or urbanization. Economic life is still based on mixed agriculture and local marketing.

My wife and I lived both in the town of Jimma and in the hills near Jiren and were participant observers of the life of the community there. We could not observe for ourselves the operation of the kingdom, the life of the court, and the process of appointment, but the memory of the kingdom remains strong among the people of Jimma, and it was not difficult to find men and women who had grown up under and served in the administration of Abba Jifar II, Jimma's last king. Most of the material regarding the organization and history of the monarchy is derived from interviews with older people of Jimma, especially those who lived near the palace and had some access to it. My interpreters were primarily local Galla youths who had high-school educations and spoke English and Galla. Two of them were from families prominent in political and religious affairs, and thus were able to suggest leads, allay the suspicions of potential informants, and serve as informants themselves.

Among my principal informants were an eighty-year-old former *k'adi* (Islamic judge) who had held that post for many years; an old man who had been Abba Jifar's personal body servant; the seventy-year-old grandson of the man who introduced Islam to the court of Abba Jifar I; an elderly farmer and ex-merchant whose family was close to the palace; and a nephew of Abba Jifar II who still holds a position as a subgovernor.

A reconstruction of events and structures now at least thirty, and perhaps as much as one hundred, years old obviously cannot be as full or as definite as one would wish it to be. On the other hand the information sought was straightforward. Such subjects as the powers and activities of officials, the powers of the king, and the symbols of the monarchy are not particularly sensitive or subjective, and there was little reason to distrust responses on political grounds. In order to assure as much accuracy as possible, the same questions were asked repeatedly of different informants.

On a number of important points the writings of Europeans who traveled through Jimma on and off from 1840 to 1927 have provided welcome corroboration of the statements of informants. Four accounts have been especially useful—those of Enrico Cerulli, a scholar, and Jules Borelli and Leopoldo Traversi, explorers, whose visits in Jimma were brief but whose purpose was specifically to acquire information about the kingdom, and that of Cardinal Guglielmo Massaja, who spent thirty-five years in Galla territory as a missionary. Their accounts provide an over-all picture of life and events in southwestern Ethiopia during the period. In regard to Jimma they are particularly useful in that they sometimes substantiate informants' memories of such details as the names of officials or members of the kings' families. In many cases I have given citations of travelers' accounts to add to the primary source, the word of informants. I look upon the written sources as added confirmation, but most of the material is derived from field research.

The Galla language (*afan* Oromo) is an unwritten one and has never been standardized for scholarly work or other publication purposes. The orthography employed in this study does not pretend to be a linguistic analysis, but represents this writer's hearing of the language. However, except for the addition of signs for two vowels, this system agrees closely with that which M. M. Moreno described in his book *Grammatica della Lingua Galla.* Words of Arabic origin are rendered as pronounced in Jimma.

Galla contains few sounds, other than the glottalized consonants, which present difficulties for speakers of English, and few special symbols have been used. The vowels are pronounced roughly as follows: *a* as in *father, e* as in *say* (Italian: *sera*), *i* as in *feet* (Italian: *ricco*), *o* as in *tote* (Italian: *rosso*), *u* as in *lunar* (Italian: *luna*), *ĕ* as in *bet, ĭ* as in *bit, ŭ* as in *but.* Glottalized consonants are indicated by the presence of an apostrophe directly after the consonantal sign: *k', t', p', c'; d'* represents a retroflex voiced stop; and the alveopalatals *č, š,* and *ž* are marked by the inverted circumflex, thus *č* as in *chin, š* as in *she,* and *ž* as in *vision.*

In Jimma, young boys are given Muslim names (Fakir, Yasin, Muhammad), but are renamed by the time they get married. Their mature names are generally composed of the word *abba,* "father," "owner of," plus a word descriptive of a horse. For example, Abba Jifar means "Owner of the Dappled Horse"; Abba Magal, "Owner of the Bay"; Abba Digga,

"Owner of the Demolisher." In order to identify a person more certainly the Galla refer to him by his own "horse name" followed by that of his father: Abba Garo-Abba Bok'a, Abba Jifar-Abba Gommol, and so on. Titles of officials are compounded by using *abba* with a word descriptive of the function. For example, *abba dula,* "father of war"; *abba gaba,* "father of the market"; and *abba gĭndo,* "father of the stocks" (jailer).

A GALLA MONARCHY

Jimma Abba Jifar, Ethiopia

1830–1932

I

African kingdoms and monarchical rule

The process of monarchical rule involves control over people through the intermediary of an administrative staff. Political control is impossible without a body of officials and followers who are loyal, in some measure, to the ruler; otherwise no man can be certain that his orders will be obeyed. But the very process of recruiting and rewarding followers, and delegating to them authority over people, revenue, and armed men, inevitably involves some loss of control by the monarch. There is a dynamic competition between the ruler and the officials subordinate to him. As Max Weber put the problem, "We always meet with a *struggle* between the political or hierocratic lord and the owners or usurpers of prerogatives, which they have appropriated as status groups. The ruler attempts to expropriate the estates and the estates attempt to expropriate the ruler."[1]

The struggle between the king and his administrative staff (and other forces within the society) may take different forms, but all involve the limitation of the powers and the will of one party or the other. In some monarchies the balance of power seems to reside (at a given point in time) with the officials, "barons," chiefs, generals, or leaders of corporate descent groups. Such monarchies have frequently been called "decentralized," "feudal," "segmentary states," or "federative states." But where a monarch successfully limits his subordinates and subjects by maintaining control over the economic and military resources vital to administration and political control, and has the power to appoint officials of his own choosing, we have a regime which can be called "despotic" and "centralized."

Despotism in this case does not mean "illegitimate exercise of great power" or brutality but rather ". . . unlimited authority [read "power"], a situation where the institutional restraints upon the ruler's power are at a minimum. . . . It is recognized, of course, that despotism is always a matter of degree, that complete arbitrariness on the part of the ruler is never institutionalized."[2]

Although some despotic states (and Jimma Abba Jifar in particular) may readily be classified with Southall's "unitary

1 Weber, 1948: 298. In a book which appeared after this work was completed, S. N. Eisenstadt (1963) emphasizes and elaborates upon a number of points similar to ones made in this chapter. He is partly concerned with the position and policies of rulers vis-à-vis bureaucrats and status groups in "historical bureaucratic empires" of Europe and Asia. It is noteworthy that the same generalizations seem to hold equally well for African monarchical systems.

2 L. A. Fallers, 1959: 11. This concept is different from G. P. Murdock's "African despotism" (1959: 35–39). Murdock feels that "the states of Negro Africa appear essentially as similar as the peas in a single pod" and that they strongly parallel Wittfogel's "Oriental despotism." I believe that, in spite of the numerous similarities among African kingdoms, there are basic and significant differences among them and that the term "despotism" should be reserved for those monarchies which are highly centralized. The majority of African kingdoms were not despotic by this definition.

states"[3] or Vansina's "despotic kingdoms"[4] in a typological series, I want to avoid a typological approach and to think, instead, in terms of a dynamic situation, with despotism representing a condition or state of being rather than a type of government. Centralized control may be attained by monarchs working within very different governmental structures. While some systems may be more conducive to central control than others, there seem to be conditions under which and methods whereby able rulers in many types of monarchies may gain an approximation of absolute power at least temporarily. For examples we have the success of Shaka among the nineteenth-century Zulu, of several rulers of Ashanti, of William the Conqueror in England, and of the counts of Flanders during the eleventh century.[5] We do not find despotism consistently associated with any one set of structural characteristics and there are, empirically, a great number of possible combinations of politically significant structures and practices. (This wealth of possibilities is probably one important reason that scholars have had such difficulty extending the usage of the term "feudal" to societies outside of medieval western Europe. Many polities have, at one time or another, shared some of the traits of western European feudalism without sharing quite enough to satisfy everyone.) Even a single system may combine several principles for recruiting high officials (for example, achievement, membership in particular kin groups, personal loyalty to the ruler), several methods of rewarding officials (salaries, fiefs, benefices, tax farming), and several types of armed forces (mercenaries, an age-graded militia, on-the-spot recruits). Cross-cutting these are the various ways in which local groups can be organized (as corporate villages, on the basis of descent groups, or as open-country neighborhoods) and various ways of organizing the status groups of a society—as endogamous occupational and ethnic groups, as wealth-

3 Southall, 1956: 260.
4 Vansina, 1962: 332.
5 Stephenson, 1942: 80–85.

based classes, or as "royal" and "commoner" descent groups. Many permutations of these elements are possible and there seems to be relatively little determinism in their combination.

The fortunes of rulers of any one dynasty may fluctuate considerably and there may even be cycles during which a polity alternates between periods of great central power and periods of relative decentralization. This was true, for example, of Egypt, China, Abyssinia, and the Islamic states of the Near East.[6] Vansina has suggested that the "degree of centralized control" might serve as a major criterion in a classification of African states,[7] but because such power may fluctuate readily and greatly I hesitate to use it to establish a typology. It may be appropriate to view central power along a continuum, and any particular state might be seen to vary within certain limits along such a scale.

All monarchs are faced with certain standard and minimal problems of rule, and the degree of centralization maintained in any one state depends upon the success of the king in overcoming them. Since monarchies may have many different socio-economic and structural bases these problems vary in form from place to place and a particular king will be forced to operate within the limits of certain traditions, resources, and social structure. Not all monarchs are equally endowed by their societies. European kings, for example, did not usually have to contend with the limitations imposed by corporate descent groups, whereas in Africa these were very often a vital source of difficulty for a king. In the following pages we shall consider some of the major variables involved in the maintenance of despotic control. The most important of these are the systems of appointment, of revenue collection, and of military recruitment and organization.

6 For Africa, see Gluckman's suggestions, 1963: 36–37.
7 Vansina, 1962: 331.

Appointment of officials

If a king is to remain the master of his administration he must be largely unlimited in his choice of officials and must maintain more or less direct control over the men who represent or administer the sub-groups within his society. If these officials have the traditional right to hold certain offices, or to control economic and military resources, or to maintain their own followings, the ruler may be checked in a variety of ways. There are three major types of potential checks on a ruler's freedom to appoint, transfer, and dismiss subordinates.

(1) In many African monarchies kings must deal with politically important corporate descent or residence groups which may own land, maintain political consciousness and functions, and have the right or power to insist upon the appointment to high office of their own traditional or chosen leaders. Under these circumstances the king's authority is limited and the subordinate, with his own following, can be an important political force. The numerous sources of conflict between central monarchical institutions and active lineages have been the subject of much research and discussion in recent years,[8] and Fallers suggests that "lineages are the commonest sources of political pluralism in African kingdoms—the commonest sources of political sub-structure capable of limiting the authority of rulers and of providing media of political expression for social sub-groups."[9]

Even within a system of important corporate lineages, however, a shrewd and active king may obtain considerable success by appointing new military or administrative officials and by balancing groups and their leaders against each other thus cross-cutting the power of the lineages. In Buganda a major element in the growing power of the king throughout

8 For example, L. A. Fallers, 1956, 1963; Southall, 1956; Fortes, 1960; and Smith, 1956.
9 L. A. Fallers, 1963: 322.

the nineteenth century was the progressive elimination of hereditary clan heads from positions of political importance, and their replacement by the personal choices of the king.[10] Although Ashanti never became as highly centralized as Buganda, the king was able to check the power of regional sub-chiefs by appointing personal followers as military governors over newly conquered lands and strengthening the military position of the capital (Kumasi). And a king may also count on the sub-chiefs to help him check the threat from the military chiefs.[11] As long as such corporate groups and their leaders exist, however, they pose a potential threat to the autonomy of the ruler.

(2) Frequently a monarch is enmeshed in a lineage system of his own, of such strength that its members can demand rights to certain positions and estates, and a share of the decision-making at the top level of government. This may lead to the fragmentation of the monarchy, as well as to the loss of the monarch's autonomy. Richards has discussed this problem in some detail with respect to certain African states.[12] She points out that while royal relatives may form a group of supporters for the king, they also frequently share with him his aura of ritual importance and qualification to rule. By virtue of their exalted position in the (often sanctified) descent line of the king they may, if given responsible positions far enough away from the center of the kingdom, break away and establish their own dynasties. This process has been documented among the Ngoni,[13] and the Basuto.[14] Such monarchs as those of Swaziland,[15] Burundi,[16] and Shambala[17] were bound to appoint their own close kinsmen to the most important positions in the land.

10 Richards, 1960: 35–36; Southwold, n.d.
11 Tordoff, 1962.
12 Richards, 1961.
13 Barnes, 1954.
14 Richards, 1961.
15 Richards, 1961.
16 Albert, 1960.
17 Winans, 1962.

In addition, it was common in Africa for the queen mother or one of the king's sisters to hold an institutionalized position of great ritual, political, and judicial importance, as, for example, among the Swazi, Jukun, and Ashanti.

(3) In Africa, as in Europe and Asia, administrators and chiefs are frequently given grants of land over which they have economic as well as governmental power. Holders of fiefs and estates time and again manage to build up wealth and entrench themselves locally. They may get strong enough to demand that their sons succeed to their offices and to the rewards that go with them. While one man alone may be too weak to resist the king, a group of such officials or nobles may band together to prevent the king from setting a precedent they consider threatening to their interests. Weber was concerned with the development of "status groups" of fief or benefice holders in Europe and Asia. There are examples of this phenomenon in Africa as well. Beattie has documented this process for traditional and modern Bunyoro,[18] and it was a problem for the kings of Abyssinia, Nupe, and Buganda.

The task of the king is to discourage the inheritance of such positions. He may shift men from region to region in an effort to discourage "the formation of local groups loyal to the administrator personally."[19] or may disperse a man's holdings throughout the kingdom rather than let them be concentrated in one area. (This was the policy of William the Conqueror.[20]) Another possibility is to hold out promise of progressively larger benefices in return for loyal service, as was the practice in Buganda.[21] If all other policies fail, the powerful ruler will purge the sons of the late governor and replace him with a man of his own choosing. This was a common occurrence in

18 Beattie, 1960; 1961.
19 Southwold, n.d.: 3.
20 Stenton, 1951: 65.
21 Colson, 1958: 47.

the Islamic empires of Iraq and Persia, and was found in nineteenth-century Buganda and Nupe in Africa.

The monarch's aim is always to appoint officials dependent upon him alone, who will thereby be easier to control. Among the potentially tractable followers of the king are affines, slaves

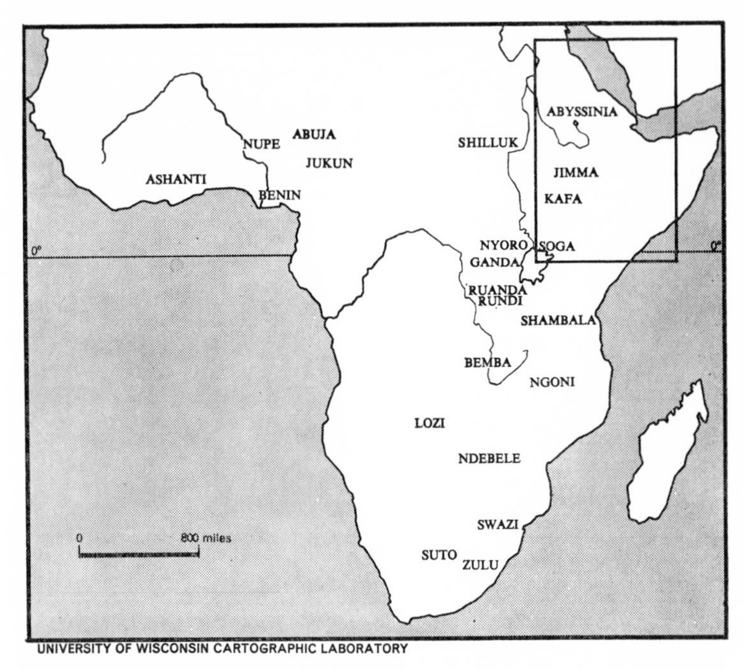

Map 1. African kingdoms mentioned in the text

and eunuchs, foreign mercenaries, and, sometimes, commoner "clients." The ruler tries to check hereditary nobles and play individuals and interest groups against one another in order to maintain his own freedom of action. As M. C. Fallers remarks of the states of Busoga and Buganda, "rulers always attempted to balance the authority of princes, who shared the royal ascribed 'fitness-to-rule,' with that of commoner appointees loyal to themselves personally."[22]

22 M. C. Fallers, 1960: 67.

Organization of administrative activity

It is in the king's interest to maintain as direct control as possible over the functions performed by his government. Above all, it is vital that control over economic resources and armed forces does not become so diffused throughout the political system that the ruler cannot keep an effective monopoly over them.

Revenue collection

All rulers must collect revenue of some kind and maintain the right to extract corvée labor. (Revenue frequently comes from personal or property taxes, market taxes and tolls, court fines, and trade monopolies.) Rulers need material wealth to provision palaces, support builders and artisans, reward servants and followers, pay the bridewealth for many wives, and exhibit generosity to subjects in times of trouble or celebration. Economic goods make a monarch's life pleasant and impress his subjects, but above all they give him a fund to draw upon in order to pay for services and to meet responsibilities. The greatest single need is for resources to support administrators and military forces. Here the monarch faces a major dilemma, for the administrators he has to remunerate are generally the people on whom he must rely to collect the revenue. Thus the problem of remuneration of officials is inseparable from that of revenue collection. Traditional monarchs have found only a limited number of solutions to these problems. Basically, the ruler may try to collect most of the revenue himself and then give it to his officials, or he may allow them to collect their own wealth.

According to Weber, "the patrimonial retainer may receive his support in any of the following ways: (a) By maintenance at the table and in the household of his chief; (b) by allowances from the stores of goods or money of his chief, usually primarily allowances in kind; (c) by rights of use of land in return for service; (d) by the appropriation of property income, fees, or taxes; (e) by fiefs."[23] Although this was written without consideration for African states, it was as true of them as of European or Asian states. Benefice lands were found in Buganda and Barotseland, fiefs in Abyssinia and Nupe, and tax-farming in Abyssinia.

If a king is able to maintain his followers directly from his own resources they will be most dependent upon him. However, as Bendix remarks, "such maximum control militates against effective government over a large territory, because the cost involved readily exceeds the personal resources of even powerful rulers."[24] When officials are rewarded with grants of land or the right to collect taxes from a region, they gain in independence from the king. They may acquire their own following and dependents, or exploit their lands so successfully as to gain great economic power. And, in practice, there is a constant tendency for such rights to become inheritable, encouraging the development of local dynasties. The alert monarch, then, must constantly promote and demote (a process well known to Abyssinians as *šum-šir*, "appoint-dismiss"), enlarge and diminish, expropriate and reallocate estates.

Administrators who are supported through estates or rights to an income from taxation generally collect the taxes from the people under them directly, and then send a certain sum to the king. In this case the official invariably attempts to extract as much revenue as possible from those beneath him, while withholding as much from his superior as he feels he can get away with. Not infrequently the royal treasury becomes considerably depleted, as not enough revenue reaches it. Nadel reports the occurrence of this phenomenon in Nupe, and of consequent military campaigns to check the too-independent nobles.[25] Monarchs may attempt to check the revenue collec-

23 Weber, 1947: 351.
24 Bendix, 1960: 347.
25 Nadel, 1942: 118–19.

tion of their administrative officials by appointing special tax collectors and census takers. (In this case the hope is that losses from bribery will be less than those incurred through other forms of collection.)

Military recruitment

In all states there is some form of armed force at the command of the ruler. The manner in which this force is organized, its loyalties allocated, its recruitment and mobilization effected, however, varies from state to state. Two major possibilities are (*a*) to call upon local chiefs or vassal followers to recruit, possibly equip and maintain, and lead levies of troops; (*b*) to attempt to control a centralized force, loyal primarily to the ruler rather than to other officials.

The classic example of the dependence of the ruler upon the levies of his vassals is, of course, found in medieval Europe. When men are granted land specifically in order to maintain and equip fighting forces, the position of the monarch is at its most precarious, for he has few means to insure the reliability of these troops, whose primary loyalty and dependence is to their immediate chief. Risky or not, however, kings in many areas have employed this method, especially in frontier areas and in states which are in the process of enlarging themselves militarily. In Nupe, for instance, "the ever expanding kingdom, increasingly dependent upon the military help of the nobility, had to secure their services more and more by granting them landed property in the form of fiefs, and thus investing them with a portion of territorial sovereignty."[26] The same was true of Abyssinia until the twentieth century, and even in highly centralized Buganda the monarch allowed officials living on the border to maintain troops on grants of land. There is an intimate relation between military leadership, rights over land on which to support troops, and the consequent increase in the territorial independence of the officials.

26 Nadel, 1942: 121.

Where kinship units and local groups are important and have corporate leadership, armed forces may exist on the local level under traditional leadership. A good example of this form of organization was the Ashanti confederation, where, in addition to the king's own troops, each community and each territorial region was organized for war.[27]

In an effort to acquire absolute control, a king will frequently use his own resources to support a force of mercenaries—foreign or local—to act as a personal bodyguard and the nucleus of the country's army. By placing them under the command of a favorite official, and by reimbursing them directly (with a salary, stores, or even grants of land), he hopes to retain their loyalty. Slaves have been called upon to serve in the ranks and as officers in Africa (for example, nineteenth-century Abuja[28]) as well as in Byzantium and the Ottoman Empire. (As Machiavelli and Weber pointed out, great dependence upon mercenaries can also lead to unhappy consequences for the ruler.) The strength of Zulu and Swazi rulers was enhanced in no small measure by their leadership of national standing armies. These armies were divided into regiments based on age-grades, and their units were so placed and commanded as to increase their dependence upon the central authorities rather than on the local commanders and chiefs.[29]

The aura of kingship

An aura of supernatural power, even divinity, has often been associated with African rulers, from ancient Egypt to Haile Selassie I, and from Ashanti to Swaziland. There can be little doubt that this element may aid a king in maintaining his position. Richards has noted that the ritual status of a king (such as the king of Swazi) may give him vital preëminence

27 Rattray, 1929.
28 Smith, 1960.
29 Kuper, 1946: 15; Gluckman, 1940: 32.

over all pretenders.[30] The Pharaohs of Egypt represent a combination of divine monarchs and despots. On the other hand, it is clear that there is no correlation between divinity and despotism. The king of the Shilluk was a prime example of divine kingship, but his political power has been seriously questioned,[31] whereas the Kabaka of Buganda, whose supernatural aura was minimal, was one of the most despotic rulers in Africa.[32] Meek has pointed out that the king of the Jukun was so hedged about by taboos and surrounded by priests that he was almost a prisoner of his own divinity.[33]

If the concept of the sacredness of the king was neither a universal nor a necessary accompaniment to kingship in Africa, it was, nevertheless, a very old and widespread cultural complex of great importance. It is likely that every state in sub-Saharan Africa contained at least a few of the characteristics of the ideal African divine monarchy.[34]

The strategy of monarchical rule

In order to succeed in the struggle with his administrators, a king must wherever possible apply techniques designed to control them. His aim must always be to limit the scope for independent action of his officials. One means to this end is to restrict each subordinate to as small a sphere of operation as is practical in any particular case. The more limited and closely defined is the jurisdiction of any individual, the more dependent he will be.

An "all-purpose chief" is always a potential threat to a king. Such a chief may have his own army, collect his own taxes,

30 Richards, 1961.
31 Evans-Pritchard, 1948.
32 Wrigley, 1959: 37–38.
33 Meek, 1931: 333–34.
34 Greenberg, 1949.

and maintain his own court and grand style of life. Richards gives examples of this from among some Bantu peoples:

> Accepted as a royal, the Bantu prince tends to set up in royal style in his distant province. His village is built as a small replica of the capital; his officials have similar duties and titles; he begins to accumulate regalia of his own and sometimes to imitate the rituals of the central kingship. . . .
>
> . . . Established as a governor for the king some fifty to a hundred miles away, what more likely than that the prince should strive to become a kinglet?[35]

Such a chief may be sufficient unto himself. If he can acquire a large enough following he can simply remove his region from the central state and establish it as an independent realm. (According to Barnes, this was the process by which the Ngoni states were constantly fissioning and spreading.[36]) But a regional governor who may not levy taxes or lead armed men will be forced to rely upon the operations of many others. Where a kingdom is highly organized in terms of its economic life, public works, military aspects, and trade, the powers of its officials are fragmented and their dependence upon the central integrating element, in this case the king, is increased. In the following passage Richards describes the administration of Buganda:

> . . . clan heads, king's favourites and warriors competed for office at the Kabaka's pleasure. The king appointed governors to administer districts and then gave fiefs or benefices in the same districts to men who rendered service directly to him, and not to the appointed governor. Finally he appointed his own army head over a series of divisional captains who collected their own local troops for a central army, in addition to the county forces collected by governors as part of their customary service. Thus the system consisted of a series of separate but overlapping pyramids of authority all centered on the monarch. . . . At the district level the members of each hierarchy spied on representatives of other

35 Richards, 1961: 143.
36 Barnes, 1955.

hierarchies and obtained favour by betraying rival dignitaries to the king.[37]

The Lozi of Barotseland offer another striking case of a centralized state in which there are a number of pyramidal hierarchies all culminating in the king. Among the Lozi administration and allegiances were so organized that hardly any two kinsmen or neighbors belonged to the same groups. Everyone was constantly joining different groups with different leadership and membership and it was thus impossible for any man outside of the palace to gain anyone else's undivided loyalties.[38]

Other common techniques used by monarchs to strengthen their control range from the appointment of officials with overlapping jurisdiction to less subtle means such as demanding frequent appearances of officials at court—common in Bunyoro and twentieth-century Ethiopia as well as Louis XIV's France, or moving the court to potential trouble spots—a practice employed by the monarchs of Abyssinia as well as by William the Conqueror.

Despotism may have a number of different origins. If a ruler is able to gain control over his appointments, put bounds to the influence of his own and other kinship groups, and personally direct the collection of revenue and the mobilization of armed forces, he will be able to gain "total power." The hypothesis that these steps are more readily accomplished in "hydraulic societies" or "bureaucratic systems" than in other types of political systems—those based on firm kinship ties or on the concept of feudal land tenure, for example—is not necessarily being questioned here. I do suggest, however, that there are numerous roads to despotism, and, moreover, that no dynasty is indefinitely immune to decentralization and the breakdown (at least temporarily) of the monarch's control.

37 Richards, 1960: 350.
38 Gluckman, 1951.

In the following chapters I shall be dealing with the state of Jimma Abba Jifar in which despotism was given a head start because of some of the pre-monarchical traditions of the western Galla.

II

Historical and ethnic background

The Galla of Ethiopia,[1] Somalia, and Kenya speak a language of the eastern branch of the Cushitic language family, a sub-group of the Afro-Asiatic language family. Most of the Cushitic languages, of which there are at least seventy-five, are found in Ethiopia and its immediate border regions, and save for several Semitic languages, known to be recently intrusive, and a few Nilo-Saharan languages on the western and south-

1 The name "Ethiopia" will be used to refer to the whole region and to the modern state (since 1890). "Abyssinia" denotes the major kingdom of the north which was a distinct polity during the Middle Ages. The "Abyssinians" are the Semitic-speaking peoples of the northern regions, especially the Amhara and Tigre of Eritrea, Tigre, northern Shoa, Gojam, Lasta, and Begemder (Map 2).

ern borders, all the languages of Ethiopia are Cushitic. This close correlation between Ethiopia and the Cushitic languages, and the great proliferation of these languages, suggest that Cushitic-speaking peoples have lived in this area for a long time.

Early Ethiopian history

It is generally assumed that Ethiopia's peoples have been agriculturalists for several thousand years.[2] Today sedentary mixed agriculture is the rule, although there are important groups of cattle and camel pastoralists in the lowland border areas surrounding the Ethiopian plateau on all sides. The plow is widely used and grains are of basic importance, especially in the north. The most important grains are t'ef (an indigenous domesticate), sorghum and millets, wheat, and, today, maize. In the southwest the hoe often replaces the plow and the staple crop is *ensete edule,* the "false banana," also a local domesticate. Since there has been practically no prehistoric archaeology done in Ethiopia, it is impossible to determine the age of these traits. Neither do we know anything of the social or political systems of the early Cushites.

Sometime in the first millennium B.C. groups of immigrants speaking Semitic languages came to Ethiopia from South Arabia, in those days the seat of the little-known civilizations of Mina, Saba, and Himyar. The immigrants settled in the north, where they presumably mixed with the indigenous population who are believed to have been people related to the contemporary Agau Cushites of northern Ethiopia. Orientalists have assumed that it was the Semites who introduced the use of metals, the plow, weaving, and new types of plants and animals.[3] As Simoons points out, these are conjectures without evidence to support them and they seem doubtful.[4] It is

2 Murdock, 1959; Simoons, 1960.
3 Trimingham, 1952: 33.
4 Simoons, 1960: 14.

equally uncertain just how much influence the Semitic speakers had on political and social life.

In Tigre and Eritrea the immigrants evidently introduced forms of irrigation and water control, the use of writing, and advanced techniques of stonework and building. They may also have been responsible for the presence of certain South Arabian religious concepts found in Ethiopia. In the north of Ethiopia the Semitic-language speakers gained an ascendancy which they have held ever since. Their first kingdom, Aksum, was founded before the Christian era. Taking advantage of its proximity to the Red Sea and the Sudan, Aksum became peripherally involved with the Mediterranean world through trade and the exchange of emissaries. It was in contact with the Greeks and Ptolemaic Egyptians. Through its connections with the Mediterranean, Aksum was exposed to Christianity very early and adopted it about A.D. 330. This event gave a unique stamp to the culture of northern Ethiopia.

Throughout the first few centuries A.D. Aksum prospered. But in the seventh century Islam arose across the Red Sea and a series of struggles between the Muslims and the Christians began. One eventual result was the isolation of Aksum from the Red Sea trade through the loss of its ports to the Muslims. The decline of trade, the lessening of contacts with the outside world, and troubles with subject peoples internally, all seem to have weakened Aksum, and in time the center of gravity of Ethiopian civilization shifted further south to areas occupied by the Amhara, speakers of another Semitic language. There, in the regions of Lasta, Amhara, and Shoa, the new Christian kingdom of Abyssinia arose.

During the fifteenth and sixteenth centuries, with the expansion of the Portuguese, there were renewed contacts between Ethiopia and the countries to the north. Contemporary accounts picture the kingdom of Abyssinia as relatively wealthy but provincial, ruled by powerful kings who controlled many provinces and tributary states with varying degrees

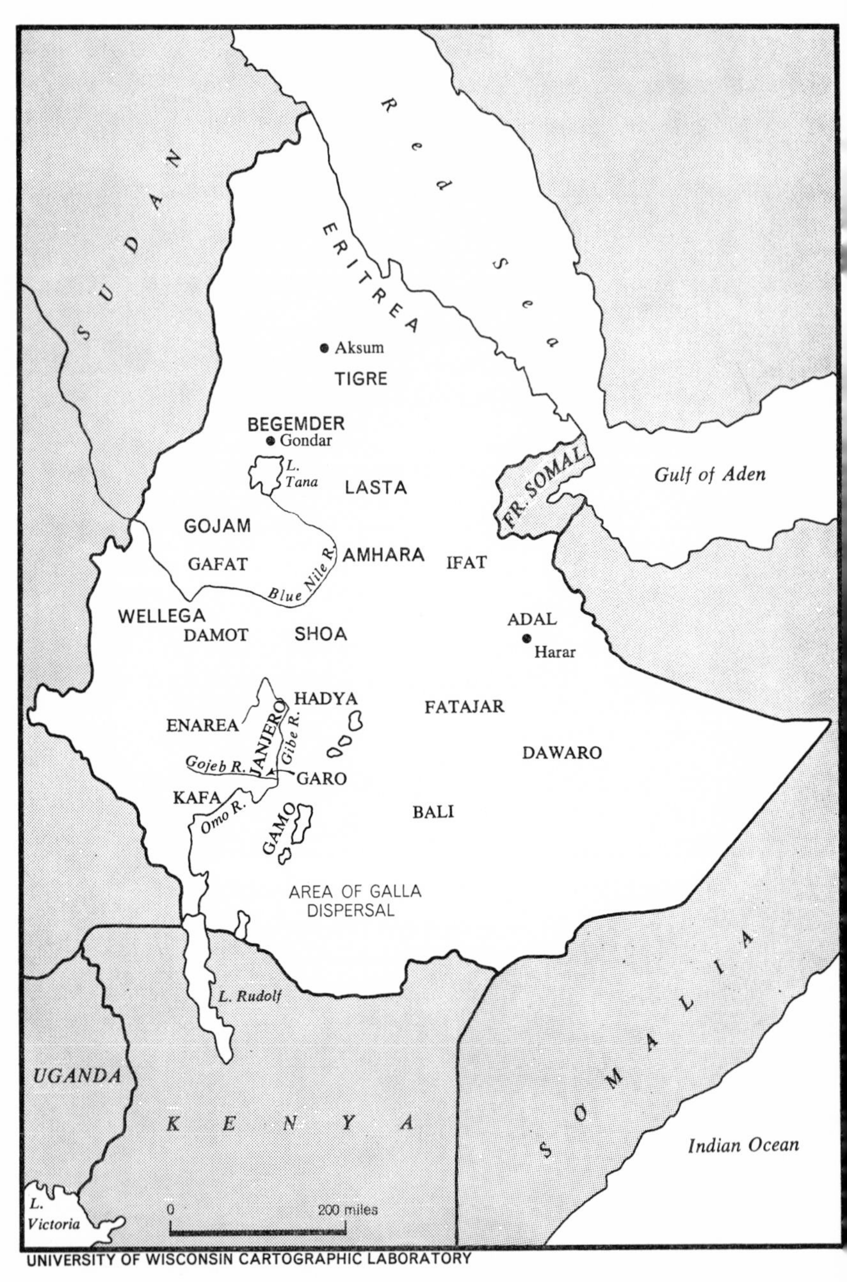

Map 2. Ethiopia at the time of the Galla migrations, sixteenth century

of success. To the east and south of the Abyssinians there were a number of smaller states, some Muslim and others pagan. The Muslim states of Ifat, Bali, Adal, Hadya, Dawaro, and Fatajar may have owed their formation to stimuli from Arabia and the coastal states along the Horn of East Africa. Possibly the pagan, Western-Cushitic–speaking kingdoms of Enarea, Kafa, Janjero, Gamo, and Damot were formed as a result of interaction with the Abyssinian monarchy, or they may have had roots reaching further back in time. At various times in history the Abyssinians were able to control these kingdoms, demand tribute from them, and even appoint Abyssinian governors to rule them. At other times these smaller kingdoms enjoyed temporary independence. (When the central government was weak many of the original northern provinces also broke away under their own rulers.)

In the sixteenth century the Abyssinian empire was considerably weakened and reduced in size as a result of long and costly wars. About 1530 the Muslims of Adal, having recently acquired firearms from the Turks, began attacking Abyssinia. They overcame the armies in the outlying tributary states to the east of Abyssinia, and then continued into Shoa, Lasta, and Tigre, causing tremendous devastation. In 1543, with the aid of Portuguese musketeers, the Abyssinians routed the major Muslim force, and the Muslim leader was killed. The lost tributary states were not recovered until late in the nineteenth century, however, for during the sixteenth century the Galla people began to invade and occupy southern and eastern Ethiopia.

The Galla invasion

We do not know why the Galla suddenly became mobile and aggressive, but we do know from several early written sources that by 1540 the Galla had begun to attack the state of Bali. Defeating Bali, they rapidly moved on to Dawaro, Fatajar, Ifat, and Adal. Turning west, they cut off the southwestern tributaries from contact with the Abyssinians and occupied the central western region of Wellega. Said Ludolphus in 1682, "after their Irruption out of Bali, they made themselves Masters of the Provinces of Gedman, Angota, Dawara, Wed, Fata-

TABLE 1

Important Dates in the History of Ethiopia and Jimma Abba Jifar*

300 B.C.(?)–A.D. 700	The kingdom of Aksum
A.D. 330	Aksum converted to Christianity
700–1000	Decline of Aksum
1100–1300	Rise of kingdom of Abyssinia and of Islamic states
1527–1543	Period of Muslim invasions
1540	Beginning of Galla invasions of Ethiopia
1750	Galla conquest of the territory of Jimma
1750–1855	Period of Abyssinian decentralization
1800–1830	Founding of the kingdom of Jimma Abba Jifar under Abba Magal
1830	Reign of Abba Rebu, son of Abba Jifar
1830–1855	Reign of Abba Jifar I, son of Abba Magal
1855	Re-emergence of Abyssinian power
1855–1859	Reign of Abba Rebu, son of Abba Jifar
1859–1862	Reign of Abba Bok'a, son of Abba Magal
1862–1878	Reign of Abba Gommol, son of Abba Bok'a
1878–1932	Reign of Abba Jifar II, son of Abba Gommol
1883	Abyssinia begins southward expansion
1884	Abba Jifar II agrees to pay annual tribute to Menelik II of Abyssinia
1932	Haile Selassie I assumes direct control of Jimma upon the death of Abba Jifar II

* In this table, the only entirely certain date is the last one.

gar, Ifat, Guragea, Ganza, Conta, Damota, Waleka, Bizama, part of Shewa, and many intermix'd kingdoms. Nor had they stopp'd there, had they not, being rent into Divisions among themselves, turn'd their Arms one against another . . ."[5] In time they came to dominate still other regions, such as Raya and Yeju in northeastern Ethiopia, the Gibe region (west of the Gibe and north of the Gojeb rivers) of the southwest, and Wollo and southern Shoa in central Ethiopia.

5 Ludolphus, 1682: 85.

The progress of the Galla into these regions was remarkably rapid. Within thirty years they had accomplished their major conquests and occupied perhaps one-third of the empire. Today the Galla occupy much of the best land in Ethiopia, and although they are not in continuous distribution they extend from northeastern Ethiopia to southeastern Kenya, and from the Sudan to the Somalilands.

The Galla arrived at the area west of Addis Ababa late in the sixteenth century. There they came into contact with a number of non-Galla monarchies: Gafat, Damot, Shoa, Gojam, Enarea, Janjero, Garo, and Kafa. The relations between the Galla and these kingdoms were unfriendly. Manoel Almeida's account of Fernandes' travels in southern Ethiopia in 1613 and 1614 tells of the hostility between the Galla and their neighbors in Enarea, Shoa, Gojam, Garo, and Janjero.[6] In a later period, both Krapf and Harris relate the attempts of Shoan kings to collect tribute from the Galla by means of devastating punitive expeditions. Every writer tells of constant wars between the Galla and their neighbors.

Eventually the Měč'a Galla occupied the territory west of present-day Addis Ababa from the Blue Nile on the north to the Gojeb River on the south and westward to the Didessa River. They were divided into many groups having no political unity. According to Galla folk reconstruction of history, however, they were all descended from one son, Měč'a, of a man called Raya. Raya is said to have also sired the ancestors of the Tulama and the Wollo Galla who live to the east and northeast of the Měč'a.[7]

Most writers have assumed that the Galla invaders were

6 Beckingham and Huntingford, 1954: 150–53.

7 The Galla view their history in genealogical terms. Groups in space are related to common ancestors, and their present distribution explained as the result of the movement of brothers away from each other. This might mirror the actual process, but it clearly does not mirror actual genealogical relations beyond a few generations. It is rare to find two accounts agreeing in detail, and the regional groups are generally not extended kinship groups.

solely pastoral until after the conquest. Although it is unlikely that they would have had much time or opportunity for settled farming during the more tumultuous periods of their migrations and conquests, I agree with Haberland that there is good reason to believe that the Galla were mixed agriculturalists before their expansion.[8] They evidently learned to breed and ride horses from their northern enemies and they used horses to good advantage in their wars.

It is not always possible to say what happened to the preexisting populations in the lands which the Galla conquered. Some were bypassed, possibly forced into smaller areas, and left to live among Galla groups. Others may have been driven out or absorbed. Undoubtedly both of these processes occurred. Contrary to the frequent assumption in the African literature, in no case did "conquest states" of pastoralists over agriculturalists arise; nowhere do Galla rule over non-Galla.

Galla political organization

When the Galla began their expansion they were, to the best of our knowledge, one culturally homogeneous group. Most Galla recognize a common genealogical relation and speak one mutually intelligible language. But ecology, time, and interaction with other peoples and cultures led to great diversity among Galla groups, especially with regard to political organization and religion.

Thus the socio-political organization of the western Galla must be considered from two different aspects. The first of these is the ideal pattern of the society, including forms of settlement, leadership, and descent similar to those of many of the non-monarchical peoples of Kenya and elsewhere in southern Ethiopia. The second is the pattern of political leadership which grew up through the vicissitudes of life in highland Ethiopia and which came, in time, to supplement or supersede some of the older patterns.

8 Haberland, 1963: 772–74.

The Galla of Ethiopia do not place much importance on extended kinship as the basis for social and political activity. Like the Nandi, Kipsikis, Pakot, and Kikuyu of Kenya, among others, the Galla local community, composed of people from various descent groups, forms the basic socio-political unit. Descent groups are not localized, do not own joint economic property (although property may remain in the hands of a man's lineal descendants for some generations), do not have important political leadership, and are not the foundation for intergroup relations. The nuclear or joint family is free to move and settle in communities with members of other descent groups. The local community tends to be a hillside or district with dispersed homesteads rather than a nucleated village, and the people living in the area interact regularly as neighbors. Within these communities political positions are generally based on ability and achievement rather than on descent.

Leadership in this society was ideally and formally derived from the age-grade system (*gada*). Men who were initiated at the same time remained members of a "set" throughout their lives, passing through a series of five grades or time periods, each of eight years duration. As men passed through these grades—from youth to warrior to elder—they took on more responsible leadership roles and gained in stature and importance. When a set reached the fifth grade it was said to rule the country, that is, to lead in council meetings (*č'afe*) and to arbitrate disputes. Each set elected from among its number several officials who were, theoretically, the most prestigeful men in the community.

The *abba boku* ("father of the sceptre") or *hayu* chaired assembly meetings and was the chief speaker and representative of the group. He might also be called upon to tour his territory as an arbitrator.[9] He never served for more than eight years. When a group began its tenure as the "ruling" set, the *abba boku* recited a series of "laws" (*sera*), or customary procedures

9 Isenberg and Krapf, 1843: 256.

for such things as inheritance, blood-wealth, and the treatment of artisans and strangers.

The evidence suggests that these council meetings were attended by men of a territory in varying capacities: as members of the ruling grade, as elders, as representatives of families and lineages, and as disputants. The participants argued and discussed, the *abba boku* proclaimed the will of the council, and in many cases the moral force and will of this group prevailed so that differences were peacefully settled. However, we are also told that the *abba boku* was powerless if his arguments could not convince. Soleillet noted among the Galane Galla of Shoa in the 1880's that after the formal installation ceremonies which occurred every eight years, the *hayu* "returns to his home and has very little occasion to exercise his authority . . ."[10] Cardinal Massaja reported on a meeting of the *gada* assembly under its *abba boku* in Gudru in the 1850's. It was held to compose differences between two factions, but it was powerless, not only to keep the peace, but even to enforce the payment of compensation. Massaja wrote of the *abba boku,* "Outside of the public assemblies he hasn't any authority, but is a simple private person like all the others."[11]

D'Abbadie, Salviac, and others reported that there were other elected officials who aided the *abba boku.* They mention the *abba sa'a, irresa,* and *moti (abba dula).* These terms were translated by d'Abbadie as, respectively, "chief of public finances," "grand pontif," and "chief with executive power and above all the general in times of war";[12] Salviac also mentions *dori* and *raba,* which he translates as "assessors and judges."[13] Whatever these officials did, these descriptions are probably not accurate reflections of their powers and duties within the *gada* system. Their existence does however, point up another ideal pattern among the Galla: the election of functionally

10 Soleillet, 1886: 258.
11 Massaja, 1886, III: 79.
12 D'Abbadie, 1880: 176.
13 Salviac, 1901: 183.

specific officers for the performance of different tasks.

The *gada* assemblies and officers were territorially organized institutions, uniting contiguous local districts. There is no direct evidence as to how large an area might be united in this manner, but I suspect this was partly an *ad hoc* matter. Larger or smaller districts would be represented at assembly meetings and in common political action, depending on how widespread a dispute was, how great a threat (or opportunity) an enemy posed, and the general state of political relations in a region at any time.

In most Galla areas for which we have information—Harar, Shoa, Wellega, and elsewhere—we find this ideal pattern, which might be called "republican." Political membership and leadership was based largely on common residence and on achievement ("universalistic" criteria); officers were elected; they served strictly limited terms and could not succeed themselves; and they held functionally specific positions with closely defined tasks. There was also an insistence on thrashing out problems in open council meetings.

In spite of the Galla ideals of rotation of offices and authority, there is definite evidence that Galla political life had other facets not encompassed by the *gada* system. Galla culture produced important men of wealth and power, many of whom could be independent of the *gada* system. These men arose primarily through success in warfare and through control over trade.

While the *abba boku* was greatly limited in his authority, the elected war leader, called the *abba dula* (or *moti*), was evidently not so circumscribed. Soleillet says that in time of war "the able-bodied, the warriors, gather together; they elect the *abba dula* . . . , a sort of dictator, who will command the country while the hostilities last."[14] Beke, who was in Gojam in the 1840's, reports of the Galla to the south of Gojam that "Each tribe has its own chief, ruling districts of greater or lesser ex-

14 Soleillet, 1886: 258.

tent, whose authority, it is true, is rather suited for and exercised in times of war than in those of peace, when the traditions of the nation, as preserved by the elders, and public opinion, have more to do with the government of each tribe than the will of the *abba-dula* or chief—literally *warrior*."[15]

War leadership was the major source of power in Galla society, and this had consequences for the whole social structure. Wherever we find chieftainship or kingship among the Galla, the name of the leader is invariably *abba dula* or *moti*. Furthermore, Massaja, who lived among the Mĕč'a for many years, describes an extremely revealing occurrence in Lagamara. In a war between Lagamara and Čelia (two Galla groups) a raid was led by three *abba dula*, each with his own following. Čelia suffered a complete defeat and its people fled. Normally when the spoils of war were distributed land was returned to the old owners, in return for compensation. In this case, however, the people did not come back for a while, so the three *abba dula* decided to divide the land among themselves. When the original owners returned to the land they found that they were now tenants and subjects of the three chiefs. Some of the war leaders' own followers resettled on these newly conquered lands. The Lagamara chief with the largest following was declared the first *abba dula* of Čelia.[16]

Salviac reports similar situations. He says that ". . . the warriors who distinguished themselves during the Galla invasion and the rich who buy land with cattle and with cloth possess landholdings of several hundreds or thousands of hectares."[17] These landlords, called *abba lafa* ("possessor of land") or *abba biya* ("possessor of the country"), are found all over Galla country. As Salviac suggests, many of them acquired their wealth in warfare. Salviac notes a second vital fact: land among the Galla could be bought and sold freely. In return for animals, cash, slaves, or any other medium of exchange, anyone, even a stranger, might buy land.[18]

15 Beke, 1843: 255–56.
16 Massaja, 1887, IV: 69.
17 Salviac, 1901: 195.
18 Plowden, 1868: 310; Abebe, 1957: 62–63.

Salviac continues: "Relatives, friends, kinsmen [*alliés*] come to settle on these lands as farmers [*colons*], as clients, of whom the *abba lafa* is the patron, and to whom they pay rent. Out of this flows a reciprocity of services, a permanent and sacred bond, a tight solidarity which creates a social institution of the greatest vigor. Prosperity and misfortunes are shared. The *abba lafa* treats his *colons* as brothers and protects them as his children."[19] It is clear that landless people, artisans, immigrants, conquered peoples, and relatives settled on the lands of *abba lafa* and increased their wealth and importance. The more a man increased his landholdings, the more tenants and followers he attracted.[20]

Massaja also shows us this kind of development in recounting the rise to power (in the 1850's) of Gama-Moras, who became king of the Gudru. Gama-Moras, a man whose wealth was derived from trade, drew to himself not only kin and tenants, but a small army of riflemen as well. Indeed, Salviac also tells us that "the landlords raise from among their clients little troops of volunteers to join the forces of the tribe or to march, under private command, to the defense of the estate and of wronged friends."[21] Thus, Salviac points out, "besides the political system explained above [the *gada* system], and meshing with it, there exists another social order based on property and wealth which establishes a veritable landed nobility."[22]

There was great development of landed families in northern Galla society. As we might expect, there was also emphasis on inheritance, heirs, and the adoption of heirs. Not to have a male heir was a great tragedy, and adoption of sons was extremely common and important. The traditional inheritance pattern was primogeniture, the eldest son inheriting the major portion of the father's estate.

Although there is some question as to the relation of these landowners and war-leaders to the formally constituted *gada* council and to the *abba boku*, evidently they coexisted to a

19 Salviac, 1901: 196.
20 Abebe, 1957: 62–63.
21 Salviac, 1901: 197.
22 Salviac, 1901: 195.

great extent. At times they worked together. Salviac says that the *abba lafa* and the *abba boku* made alliances. It is also clear from Massaja's reports that when a great family did not choose to obey the *gada* council, only another private force could bring it to heel. The council might try to bring moral force to bear to prevent bloodshed; and people might go to it for justice or discussion. If the council reached a unanimous agreement on an issue such as the undertaking of a war or the punishment of a trouble-maker, action could be taken by the whole group.[23] But when matters of politics, war, and leadership were involved, the council might be by-passed. Massaja writes: ". . . the assembly, not having its own force, can not actually command respect for what it decides; for this reason, the execution of its orders and wishes almost always depends on the balance of force of the parties and of the tribes who are involved in the dispute."[24]

Northern Galla socio-political organization was one in which two seemingly contradictory principles existed: a democratic, republican, gerontocratic ideal, and leadership by a military-economic ruling elite. At times the forces were balanced; in places the ideal system worked. But in some periods and areas the ruling families and their leaders became very powerful. They by-passed the formal rules, and supplied the actual political leadership. Until a man became really powerful, however, he would have to rally public support behind him. Gama-Moras, as Massaja's account shows, did not unnecessarily overrule the council's decisions; he bowed to the assembly in order to gain support. Presumably the chiefs did not rule, they led, until, as with Gama-Moras, they had so much support, elan, and power, that they could rule.[25]

23 Plowden, 1868: 309; Massaja, 1886, III: 170–76

24 Massaja, 1886, III: 172.

25 Massaja's tale of Gama-Moras shows how a wealthy man, by bringing together armed followers and controlling the major market in Gudru, made himself indispensable to the military aspirations of his own people and the economic exchange system. He began to rule when his forces (with the aid of other local people) defeated his

There were many free peasants among these Galla. Not all men were tenants or followers. For the society at large, in day-to-day conflict resolution and the application of justice, the *gada* council and *abba boku* continued to play a part. But there were other forces at work in the society beyond the official, constitutional ones: (*a*) war leaders became men of wealth and power and tended to become community leaders; (*b*) the council and its officers were not infrequently by-passed, especially when factions developed; (*c*) here and there, now and then, powerful leaders became rulers. This was a continuous process.

It is probably impossible to generalize about the size of the political units. All the evidence suggests that they were very fluid in their extent and composition. They were as large or as small as their leadership commanded or external conditions demanded. The process of fission and fusion for *ad hoc* political reasons was constant. In the 1500's, Bahrey, an Abyssinian priest, reported of the Galla: "The tribe of Hakako is composed of Abo, Harsu, Limu; the tribe of Suba is composed of Hagalababo, Čurra; the tribe of Abo [Obo] is composed of Sayo, Abono, Tum'e, Leqa. All these, when they are allied are called Mača; but when they make war they call themselves Afre and Sadača; if they are all joined with the Tulama they are called Sapira."[26]

Warfare was constant and endemic among the Galla. They fought their neighbors and each other–ethnic group against ethnic group, kingdom against kingdom, territory against terri-

---

major rival's forces. "Remaining, finally, conqueror and master of Gudru, he soon took over the government of it, confiscating the goods of the enemies and dividing them among his soldiers, and he began to rule as prince . . . of all Gudru" (1886, III: 176). After this he reorganized his realm by creating an officialdom.

26 Beckingham and Huntingford, 1954: 113. Although this account sounds like a "segmentary system" such as that described by Evans-Pritchard for the Nuer (1940b), or by L. Bohannan for the Tiv (1958), there is no reason to believe that these groups were based on descent or that the alliances and schisms were mediated by genealogical relations.

tory, chiefly family against chiefly family, and pagan against Muslim.[27] Groups united under one leader for particular battles, then turned and fought each other.

> The large tribes, divided up under the direction of several *abba boku,* observe a rule of subordination through which, in a matter of general interest, they submit to the preëminence of a superior *abba boku.* But it is not therefore less true that each tribe and sub-tribe guards its real autonomy, that the love of arms counterbalances, among the people, the instinct for federation, and that always some particularist interest breaks the bonds of amity.[28]

The principle of easy amalgamation and contraction along territorial lines evidently operated at all levels of Galla social organization. Whether for arbitration or warfare, whether involving councils and the *abba boku* or warriors and the *abba dula,* the Galla would expand to meet momentary exigencies, putting the wider group under the leadership of one person, and then divide once again, if there was no compelling reason or force to hold them together.

The rise of strong political leadership among the Galla of western Ethiopia in the eighteenth and nineteenth centuries seems to have been encouraged by certain characteristics of Galla society, as well as by the opportunity to control trade routes and the need for continual warfare against more highly organized peoples. One of these characteristics was the general freedom from descent group restrictions on recruitment to both membership and leadership of political groups. Thus the individual family was free to decide its own place of residence and its own political affiliations. Because there were no hereditary leadership positions, competent and ambitious men were not limited by status prescriptions or proscriptions but were free to gather followings from among their neighbors, friends, and dependents, as well as from their kinsmen. If a leader

27 Cerulli, 1922; Isenberg and Krapf, 1843; Massaja, 1885 *et seq;* and Plowden, 1868.
28 Salviac, 1901: 197.

could reward his followers and satisfy them through continued success, a conscious political group might result. And since land could be individually owned and did not have to be shared with the members of a man's descent group, it could be used by the leader to help support his followers. Undoubtedly these factors were conducive to the development of powerful men among the western Galla.

From time to time leaders arose who managed to maintain control over relatively large regions. Chiefly families arose in Lagamara, Lek'a K'ellem, Lek'a Sayo,[29] and Nonno.[30] In Gudru, Gama-Moras defeated his rivals and began to rule as a king. In eastern Wellega the Bëkëre family came to dominate at the expense of the *gada* officers[31] and eventually defeated all other chiefs to become supreme in their area.[32] And five Galla monarchies arose in southwestern Ethiopia early in the nineteenth century—Gomma, Guma, Limmu, Gera, and Jimma.

History of Jimma Abba Jifar

The people of Jimma claim that their predecessors in this area were the Kafa. Cerulli suggests that the Jimma monarchy was carved out of several pre-existing kingdoms.[33] It is probable that Jimma Abba Jifar occupies former territory of Enarea in the northwest, Janjero in the east, and Kafa and Garo in the south and central regions.

As Jimma consolidated into a kingdom, its neighbors from the northeast, running clockwise, were: Janjero, T'ambaro (across the Gibe River from Jimma), Kullo and Kafa (across the Gojeb River), Gera, Gomma, Limmu, and the non-monarchical Hagalo Galla. Gera, Gomma, and Limmu are inhabited

29 Cerulli, 1933: 100.
30 Cerulli, 1922: 38, 75; Massaja, 1886, IV: 177.
31 Cerulli, 1933: 120.
32 Abebe, 1957: 9–10.
33 Cerulli, 1932: 102.

by Galla. The Kafa, Janjero, and Kullo are speakers of Western Cushitic languages, each country representing a different sub-branch of that division of Cushitic, while the T'ambaro speak an Eastern Cushitic language of the Sidamo sub-

Map 3. Southwest Ethiopia in the nineteenth century, showing the location of Galla groups and kingdoms and of non-Galla groups and kingdoms

branch.[34] Thus Jimma was surrounded by eight distinct (and hostile) political groups, representing several different cultural heritages. In addition, Jimma was in contact with other Galla groups to the north and west, with the Gurage, Shoans, Gojami, and other Semites of the north, and with such Western Cushites as the Walamo, Gamo, and Konta.

Writers throughout the past one hundred years have received differing accounts of the number of Galla groups that came to Jimma. Bieber, Cerulli, Cecchi, and Massaja have respectively stated that there were five, six, seven, and ten.[35] I was told that there were nine. The question, thus framed, is probably misleading, since it suggests a finiteness to the socio-political boundaries of these groups which they probably did not possess. There was undoubtedly a continuum of local communities, united only behind the leadership of great men and war leaders. The kingdom, when it was formed, included all of those groups which its founders could control. The kingdom was not formed by an agreement among a certain number of groups; rather, a great many Galla came to this general region and some of them were eventually swept into the Jimma monarchy.

According to legend, when the Galla first came to Jimma there were nine groups which were united under the leadership of one great sorceress and "queen" called Makahore. Makahore possessed a *boku* which, when placed on the ground, caused the earth to tremble and men to fear.[36] When the Galla came to the frontiers of Jimma, Makahore set the *boku* down and the ground began to shake. The Kafa people became afraid and fled beyond the Gojeb River where they are found now. These invaders, according to their descen-

34 Moreno, 1940: 320.
35 Onneken, 1956: 81.
36 The *boku* is the sceptre possessed by the *gada* leader, the *abba boku*. To most informants in Jimma today, however, it means merely some sort of magical object, most often a box or an "ark." The *boku* is no longer in use.

dants, then took the lands which they had captured, and settled down to farm.

It is most unlikely that all the non-Galla people who had lived in Jimma before the Galla came were killed or fled to other lands. The conquest by the Galla, however, has not involved any ethnic or social separation between the first settlers and the newcomers. In contrast to areas of Fulani conquest, or to Ankole, for example, there are, in Jimma, no major group distinctions on the basis of ethnic origin. This seems to be generally true in all Galla areas, and may be one aspect of the "universalistic" nature of Galla society and culture.[37] Thus, an ethnically distinct immigrant who settled down in the Galla country, whether as an in-law of the king or as a slave or renter, was very soon given a Galla name. Even the kin group to which the kings belonged had certain branches which are said to have been derived from "men found in the forests when Diggo came to Jimma." The members of these non-Oromo[38] branches, however, are not considered to be different (today) from the Oromo.

As the Jimma Galla all grew prosperous they became unhappy with the rule of Makahore. They resented paying tribute to her and therefore plotted to destroy her power and free themselves from her control. Having accomplished this through a ruse by which she lost her virginity and thereby her power, the nine groups were free to follow their own independent courses.

37 Cerulli and d'Abbadie report a similar situation for other Mĕč'a Galla further north and west (Cerulli, 1932, I: 126; d'Abbadie, 1880: 176). Evidently in those areas the pre-Galla populations became culturally Galla, and entered the age-grade system. See also Lienhardt on the Dinka and their neighbors (in Middleton and Tait, 1958: 107–8), and Evans-Pritchard on Nuer and Dinka relations (1940).

38 The term "Oromo" is used in Jimma to denote non-Muslim Galla. Thus the conquering Galla were Oromo, but not the indigenous peoples of the area nor the Muslim Galla immigrants from the north.

Unfortunately we have no written sources referring to the early life of the Galla in the Jimma area. We cannot even be sure when they arrived, though it may have been in the early 1700's.[39] From informants and European travelers' accounts we learn of historical events and persons beginning about 1820. Before that, however, we have only a few hints.

The people say that when they disbanded, their only intergroup contact was through meetings held under a tree in a place called Hulle.[40] Here, representatives of all groups met and made laws *(sera tuma)* under the leadership of the *abba boku.* (This agrees with what we know of other non-monarchical Galla.) These groups began to have their own leaders, and several distinct and mutually hostile groups developed. Defensive trenches (*bero*) were dug to keep warring groups apart. For example, just south of Jiren there is such a *bero* that is said to have separated the Harsu group of the Dedo area from the Badi of Sak'a. Massaja, who was there in 1854, was told that there had been, some years before, ten warring principalities, each under its own *abba dula.* "Jimma Kaka formerly, and after the division of the Jimma people, was a country without central authority governed by the *abba dulas* (like the countries of Lagamara, Nonno, Gombo, Jarri, etc.), who, on the portions of territory subject to them, had power almost like princes."[41]

At first, says tradition, the Badi of Sak'a were predominant politically. Thus Jimma was often known as Jimma Badi. There were no Jimma kings, but the Badi had great wealth and power. Another group, the Diggo, who lived in Mana, began to extend their domain late in the eighteenth century. Their first move was towards the south, to Jiren, where they

39 Trimingham, 1952: 199.
40 At this period they were considered a confederation, united by an oath (*kaka*), as a result of which they were called for many years Jimma Kaka.
41 Massaja, 1889, VI: 5–6.

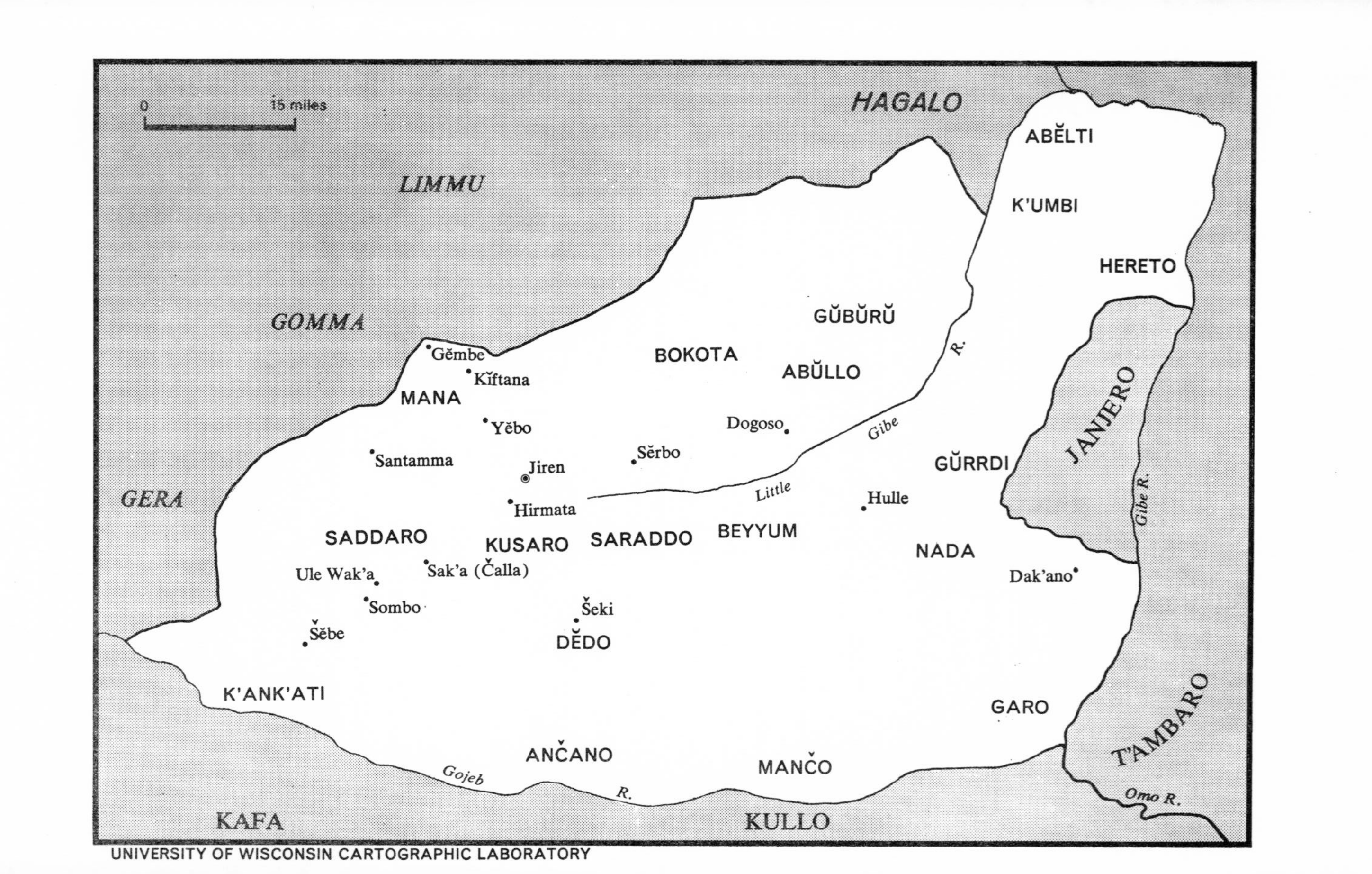
0
15 miles
HAGALO
LIMMU
GOMMA
GERA
KAFA
KULLO
ABĚLTI
K'UMBI
HERETO
JANJERO
T'AMBARO
GŬBŬRŬ
BOKOTA
ABŬLLO
GŬRRDI
NADA
GARO
MANA
SADDARO
KUSARO
SARADDO
BEYYUM
DĚDO
K'ANK'ATI
ANČANO
MANČO
Gĕmbe
Kĭftana
Yĕbo
Santamma
Jiren
Hirmata
Sĕrbo
Dogoso
Hulle
Dak'ano
Sak'a (Čalla)
Ule Wak'a
Sombo
Šĕbe
Šeki
Little
Gibe
R.
Gibe R.
Omo R.
Gojeb
R.
UNIVERSITY OF WISCONSIN CARTOGRAPHIC LABORATORY

conquered the Lalo people. By gaining the Jiren area they also obtained control of the great market and trade center at Hirmata.

At the turn of the nineteenth century a Diggo man called Abba Magal, the ruler of the Hirmata region, began a series of wars against his neighbors.[42] His sons, led by Abba Jifar I, continued these wars. They were successful in conquering much of what is now Jimma Abba Jifar. By 1830 Abba Jifar was supreme. Beke, who was in Ethiopia about 1840, wrote: "Sanna, surnamed Abba Jifar, the king of Kaka Jimma, is the most powerful of the Galla monarchs, and his dominions are very extensive, having been much enlarged by acquisitions lately made at the expense of Enarea, as well as in the south and west."[43] Thus Abba Jifar I became the first king, and the kingdom was known by his name.

As the first king, Abba Jifar must have been responsible for many administrative and political innovations. There is little specific evidence available, unfortunately, for it was not a period in which many European travelers went to Jimma. Through oral tradition it is known that he claimed the right to great areas of newly conquered lands, and to unused or virgin land. On this land he settled family, followers, and favorites. His three brothers and other companions were given administrative posts and great estates. Abba Jifar built at least five palaces in different regions of Jimma.

It was during Abba Jifar's reign—in the year 1830, according to tradition—that Jimma became Muslim. A merchant and religious man by the name of Abdul Hakim, whose home was in Gondar, came to Jimma and succeeded in converting Abba Jifar to Islam. Of Abba Jifar's role in spreading the new religion, Cardinal Massaja writes: "Embracing Islam, and declaring it the religion of the court, he called to the kingdom a quantity of Mohammedan saints to preach and to make disciples. And aiding these imposters with royal favor, very quickly the infamous religion made its way, not among the people who,

42 Cecchi, 1885, II: 540; Beke, 1843: 260.
43 Beke, 1843: 259.

having nothing to gain remained always pagan Galla, but among the chiefs, the rich, and the court . . ."[44] By 1882 most of the people of Jimma were Muslim.[45]

Abdul Hakim settled in Jiren, near the palace of the king. His tomb (*k'ubba*) is still venerated by the religious. Other Muslim traders from the north came to Jimma, and some of them were given official positions or were given land in return for their services as teachers. The council meetings at Hulle, at which elders met to arbitrate disputes (primarily involving family matters), continued during this period, and perhaps even into the beginning of the twentieth century. But with the establishment of the office of *k'adi* and the growing application of Islamic law (*sharī'a*) in matters such as inheritance and marriage, the council's jurisdiction was much reduced.

Abba Jifar died in 1855 after reigning twenty-five years. A short dispute over the succession developed between his oldest son, Abba Gommol, legitimate heir to the throne, and a younger (and more vigorous) son, Abba Rebu. Abba Jifar died in a palace east of Jiren. Abba Rebu was with him at the time, while Abba Gommol was at a palace southwest of Jiren. Abba Rebu was therefore able to gain possession of the gold ring of kingship. With his followers he reached Jiren before his brother and seized the throne. Abba Gommol was then exiled to Kafa.

Abba Rebu was an avid warrior and was constantly at war with neighboring kingdoms. His war-like spirit made him unpopular at home, for he had little patience with the wealthy who would not risk their lives and property in warfare.[46] He is said to have been tyrannical, and to have confiscated the property of wealthy men in order to bestow it on his favorite warriors. As a result his reign was cut short after four years. Massaja was told (in 1861) that Abba Rebu was killed in battle when, believing he was to meet only the forces of neighboring Gomma, he was confronted by soldiers from Limmu, Gera,

44 Massaja, 1889, VI: 10.
45 Soleillet, 1886: 165.
46 Massaja, 1889, VI: 6.

and Guma as well.[47] Informants today, however, claim that it was the Jimma people themselves who plotted to kill Abba Rebu.

Abba Rebu's son was kept from the throne because he was just an infant, and a brother of Abba Jifar I, Abba Bok'a, became king.[48] Abba Bok'a was an old man when he ascended the throne and he died (of natural causes) within two or three years, but during his short reign he did a great deal for the position of Islam in the kingdom. Massaja says that Abba Jifar and Abba Rebu were Muslims primarily for political reasons, but that Abba Bok'a was a "fanatic."[49] He built many mosques, and ordered that mosques be built in each of the sixty provinces. He sent learned Muslims to proselytize and teach in the provinces. Abba Bok'a instituted the collection of the poor tax (*zaka*), and set aside land (*wok'fi*) near Jiren, to be used by Muslim merchants (*nĕgade*) from the north who would settle there, pray at the Jiren mosques for the health of the king and the realm, and teach those who wanted to learn about Islam.

At Abba Bok'a's death there was an orderly succession as his son, whom he had designated in advance as his heir, took the throne. Abba Gommol reigned for about sixteen years, and under his direction Jimma gained in area and importance. He was responsible for extending Jimma's boundaries on the east and in 1875 he conquered Garo, the little kingdom in the southeastern corner of Jimma. Wealthy men from Jimma went to settle on land in Garo, and Abba Gommol brought important men from Garo to Jiren. Some men of the Garo royal house married into the ruling family of Jimma, and held high positions as officials of the Jimma kings. In time Garo and its people were largely integrated into Jimma.

47 Massaja, 1889, VI: 6.
48 Massaja says that Abba Bok'a became the "regent." But Abba Bok'a was ruling when Massaja traveled through Jimma, so he could not know that Abba Bok'a passed on the throne to his own son (1889, VI: 10).
49 Massaja, 1889, VI: 10.

Abba Gommol died in 1878, and his seventeen-year-old son, Abba Jifar II, became king. During his reign the northern Amharic peoples, expanding southward, finally reached the kingdom of Jimma.

The rise of modern Ethiopia

Throughout the seventeenth and early eighteenth centuries the Abyssinian kings, though reduced in the extent of their realm and in wealth, had continued to hold vital political power and had enjoyed a brief cultural renaissance at the newly founded capital of Gondar. But during the latter half of the eighteenth century the imperial power waned and there was a tendency for provincial rulers to assert their independence. New ruling houses arose in Shoa, Gojam, Tigre, Lasta, and elsewhere. (It has been asserted that one reason for the decline of the emperor's power was the establishment of a fixed capital. Before the foundation of Gondar the kings of Abyssinia lived in tent-cities which could be moved from one trouble spot to another, thus reaching many more areas directly than was possible from Gondar, which was in the northwestern part of the empire.)[50]

This period of decentralization continued until the middle of the nineteenth century when, under a series of outstanding leaders, the vigor of Abyssinia was renewed. The emperors Theodore (1855–67), John (1872–89), Menelik II (1889–1909), and the present emperor, Haile Selassie I, all strove to expand their realms and to increase their control. All sought to reduce the power of the landed nobility, and to destroy the independence of regional dynasties. To do so they used many of the classical techniques of centralization, such as establishing paid armed forces, demanding attendance of high officials at court, appointing administrators with overlapping authority, encouraging spying, and so on.

Menelik II, while he was still the king of Shoa and before

50 Trimingham, 1952: 104.

he had become emperor, began a series of military campaigns in an attempt to gain control over the regions south of Shoa, those same regions that had been lost as a result of the Galla invasions. From 1883 to 1900 his armies, supplied with new European rifles, conquered all the territory south of Shoa currently included in the modern empire. His troops defeated peoples in the borderlands who had never before been under any foreign rule. It was from these conquests (and others in the northeast and northwest) that Ethiopia's present borders were established.

Abba Jifar II

When Abba Jifar II became king the Amhara were driving towards Jimma, and Borelli, Franzoj, and other travelers accorded him little hope of retaining his kingdom for long. Through shrewd politics, however, Abba Jifar managed to keep control of his kingdom until his death in 1932.

Shortly after Abba Jifar became king, Gojami forces came to the region of the five kingdoms and caused a great deal of destruction in the neighboring areas. By 1882 the rival Shoan forces of Menelik II, under the command of Ras Gobana, had come to this area and were clearly in a position, being armed with rifles, to defeat these states in battle. Abba Jifar, realizing his predicament, agreed to pay an annual tribute to Menelik and to aid his forces in return for Jimma's continued internal autonomy. He counseled his neighbors to do likewise. But they refused and consequently suffered the devastation of their lands and the loss of their sovereignty. The Amhara now ruled them directly. Officers of the Shoan army were given land grants and allowed to live, with their soldiers, off the land and its inhabitants.[51]

Abba Jifar regularly paid tribute, generally managed to escape Menelik's anger, and enthusiastically aided Menelik in his wars against Kullo (1889), Walamo (1894), and Kafa (1897). As a result, although he relinquished certain preroga-

51 Cerulli, 1932; Perham, 1948.

tives in later years, Abba Jifar remained ruler of Jimma until his death two years after the coronation of Haile Selassie. During his reign trade flourished, agriculture and coffee-growing expanded, and Jimma and its king gained a reputation for wealth and greatness all over Ethiopia.

Because of his fifty-four year reign, and because of his remarkable personality, Abba Jifar dominates the historical memory of the people of Jimma today. Most traditions relating to the kings of Jimma and their families and governments refer to Abba Jifar II. Abba Jifar was a shrewd man and he made some innovations in the administration so as to strengthen central control of his kingdom. Nevertheless, he inherited an established monarchy and he did not substantially alter its political structure.

In 1932 Haile Selassie took over the direction of Jimma's internal affairs from Abba Jifar's grandson, Abba Jobir, who was imprisoned for failure to cooperate with the central government. Several years later the Italians came to Jimma, liberated Abba Jobir, and used him as a native governor. With the return of the Emperor to Ethiopia in 1941, however, Abba Jobir was put in jail once more. Today, having been given amnesty, he lives in what is left of the crumbling palace in Jiren, his movements circumscribed and watched.

III

Economic and community life

The primary focus of this book is the structure and operations of the government of Jimma Abba Jifar. But that government can only be understood in relation to the economic, cultural, and social setting in which it existed. It is necessary to describe this setting in order to demonstrate how the economic system could be tapped by the king, how administrators could be remunerated, why kinship groups and local communities posed little threat to the power of the king, and how geography affected Jimma's political development.

The primary source of the data was direct observation of life in Jimma in 1959 and 1960. Although it is conceivable that a few details are anachronistic, I am certain that, except where indicated, the facts presented here do reflect life in the nineteenth century. My own observations are supported by the testimony of informants as to life in the nineteenth century, written accounts (especially of economic life), and comparison with other Galla groups—especially for kinship and community organization.

Environment

Jimma is on the southern part of the Ethiopian plateau, which extends from north to south, west of the Rift Valley. It is rolling to hilly grass and forest land, but much of the forest has been cleared away for farmland. Most of Jimma is from 4,000 to 6,500 feet in altitude, in the climatic zone known to the Ethiopians as the *woina dŭga,* the "temperate middle highland."[1] There is hardly ever frost, and the daytime temperature rarely exceeds 85° F. Cultivation is possible all year round.

Jimma gets about 65 inches of rainfall per year. Although rain may fall at any time of the year, the heaviest concentration is in the two rainy seasons—July–September and February–March. A great many small rivers, variable as to water content from season to season, run through Jimma. All of them drain into the Omo River and eventually into Lake Rudolf.

Although censuses were taken by the monarchy before 1930 for the purpose of taxation, no records seem to have survived. Jimma's population otherwise has never been counted or even guessed at on any solid basis. Cardinal Massaja, in 1861, declared that Jimma had 150,000 inhabitants.[2] The Italian *Guida dell' Africa Orientale Italiana* estimated Jimma's population at 300,000 in 1936.[3] The area of the kingdom at its height (in 1875) was about 5,000 square miles.

1 Simoons, 1960: 8.
2 Massaja, 1889, VI: 6.
3 Consociazione Turistica Italiana, 1938: 528

Communications and animal transportation within the kingdom are not difficult. There are no deep, swift rivers, rugged valleys, mountains, or escarpments to divide the land. Although in the rainy season roads become muddy and slippery, caravans and riders can use the roads all year long. Thus Jimma and its neighbors are linked by routes easily traveled by men and animals.

Trade between the north and the southwest passed through Jimma, much of it carried on by Jimma merchants. Through Hirmata (where the modern town of Jimma is situated) passed caravans to the southwest (to Kafa, Maji, Gimira); the south (Kullo, Konta, Uba, and elsewhere); to the west (Gomma, Guma, Gera Ilubabor); and north to Limmu, Nonno, Shoa, Wollo, and Gondar. Jimma was thus a busy crossroads, and it received cultural influences and immigrants from all of these directions and sources. (Arabs, Indians, and Greeks also came in small numbers, especially around the turn of the century.)

Jimma's geographical environment favorably influenced the monarchy in several ways. Its fertility, climate, and good rainfall made Jimma wealthy from agricultural production. This wealth was taxed by the kings and was conducive to extensive local and long-distance trade. The trade attracted outsiders who brought foreign products and ideas. Ease of travel also encouraged trade and facilitated political communications from the palace to the borders of the kingdom.

Economic life

Landholding and access to land

The Jimma Galla are sedentary farmers, and their most vital economic resource is land. Land, whether acquired through conquest, through purchase, or through traditional and continued occupation, is owned within the patrilocal extended family. It is held and controlled by the father of a family until his death.

In Jimma a rich landowner may have one or more great parcels of land (*yĕbbo*) on which he and his followers and tenants reside. Before 1932, a rich landowner would have had slaves as well. The tenants (*k'ubsisa*) owe the landlord a fixed amount of labor or may pay rents in currency or kind. The *abba lafa* ("lord of the land") appoints stewards to see to the performance of the tenants' obligations. In the days of the monarchy, if a landowner was a government official (or desirous of becoming one) he would spend a great deal of time at the palace away from his lands, leaving them to the care of his stewards. In addition to consolidated landholdings, men may have properties in different parts of the country. The people who live on such absentee lands (*gŭfo*) pay rents to the owner or his representative.

According to Jimma traditions, when the Galla arrived in Jimma they claimed the newly vacated lands for their own. The property taken in the original conquest is called *k'abiyye* ("caught," "captured"). As the Diggo began their expansion they expropriated newly conquered lands for the use of their leaders. When the conquest was over, the Diggo, as a group, owned more land in more places than any other group. Not all private lands belonging to others were confiscated, however, and leaders of important non-Diggo families, successful warriors, and followers and favorites of the kings were given large landholdings in return for services.

Landholdings were not frozen at one point in time, nor were they obtainable only through service to the king. A man's skill and luck in farming might force him to sell his *k'abiyye*—or enable him to buy more land. Merchants who made money in trade, or craftsmen who got money from the sale of their handiwork could buy and own land. Although a foreigner had to get the king's permission to use or buy land, there were no social bars to purchase by outsiders. This ease in the purchase and transfer of land still obtains today. Different types of land tenure may be combined. A man may live on *wok'fi* land (originally given by the king in return for religious services) but own one or more *gŭfo* properties as well.[4] The absentee lands may have been bought with the profits from trading expeditions, or have been inherited. From time to time the owner goes to collect rents from the people who live on his properties and to look after any coffee trees planted there.

A common man may make a living through owning, renting, or share-cropping a number of small plots. One man may work a field of another in return for part of the crop. Two men sometimes work together on the lands of a third, or one man may help a neighbor in return for a share of the produce of a particular field. These alliances and rentals are not based on kinship ties but on convenience and good social relationships. Crop-sharing practices obtain under all circumstances of ownership: on independently owned land, on land of an *abba lafa,* and on *wok'fi* land.

Agriculture

The basis of economic life in Jimma is mixed agriculture and the basic agricultural implement is the plow. All agricultural work is done by the men. Women are rarely seen working in the fields, and they have no hand in the care of animals except to milk the cows.

Crops. The climate and the crop inventory in Jimma make it possible for the farmers to have different crops growing throughout the whole year, although no single crop has two plantings. Grains are of paramount importance and a wide variety is planted. Foremost of these, as in much of the Ethiopian highlands, is t'ef (*Eragrostis teff; t'afi*),[5] an Ethiopian domesticate. Maize (*bok'olo*) is also of great importance, espe-

4 *Wok'fi* lands are occupied by a man and his heirs as though they were hereditary. That they are not was demonstrated during our stay in Jiren. For several weeks a number of elders went regularly, every Wednesday and Friday afternoon, to the palace mosque. Word had come from the palace that they were wanted for prayers, and they were reminded that the land which they occupied was only theirs in return for their services.

5 When two foreign terms are given for a crop the first is Latin, the second, Jimma Galla.

cially as it is the one grain which is harvested and eaten during the rainy season. Sorghum (*Sorghum vulgare; bisinga*) is a major crop and, like the other grains, can be used in *injera* (a flat, sour pancake bread), in beer, in porridge, or eaten roasted. Of lesser consequence in Jimma are finger millet (*Eleusine coracana; dagusa*), wheat, barley, and rye. Other field crops include lentils, chickpeas, and taro (*Colocasia antiquorum; godarre*).

Around the edges of the fields and in the gardens surrounding their houses the people of Jimma grow many more plants. Among the main garden crops are "Galla potato" (*Coleus edulis; dĭnĭč Oromo*) sweet potato, a number of varieties of beans and peas, a form of yam, a few leafy plants, and gourds. The primary garden crop is ensete (*Ensete edule; k'oč̣o*). This plant is not as important in Jimma as it is in most of the countries of southwest Ethiopia (Gurage, Sidamo, Gimira, for instance) where it is the staple, but it does fulfill a need during the rainy season and at other periods when few grains are available.

Jimma's basic cash crop is coffee (*Coffea arabica; bunna*). Since most of this coffee is grown in the shade, it is planted under trees around the houses and fields; but wealthy landowners may keep large forested tracts for this purpose. Poorer men manage to keep enough coffee trees to get cash for the festivals, weddings, and other occasions which take place in the months after the coffee harvest in January and February. Other cash crops of lesser importance are k'at (*Catha edulis; č̣at*), tobacco, castor beans, coriander and other spices, eucalyptus trees, and, in some areas, cotton.

Irrigation and terracing, although they occur, are not practiced on any large scale in Jimma. Individual farmers sometimes take advantage of nearby streams to dig irrigation ditches, and in some hilly regions there is gullying and work on drainage, but this sort of work is done by groups of no more than four or five men. Rainfall is generally sufficient for farming needs and the only local management of water resources involves very minor work in clearing streams or damming them to make pools from which cattle can drink.

Livestock. There are few large herds of cattle in Jimma except on the lands of the very wealthy. The average farmer has only two to eight head. Oxen are used for plowing. Not many goats and sheep are kept and mules and donkeys are owned mostly by rich men and merchants. Although the stereotype of the Galla is the "cattle complex" pastoralist, the Jimma farmer treats his animals in an off-hand manner and uses them for plowing, manuring, milk, meat, and the sale of their hides and other inedible parts. One hundred years ago the horse was a vital animal for all the western Galla. Horses were used in warfare and are reported to have been quite good, capable of both speed and extended activity.[6] Now they have been largely replaced by mules in the esteem of the people, presumably as a result of Amhara influence.

Crafts and specialization

In Jimma as in most of Ethiopia and Somalia, almost all artisanry and craftsmanship is in the hands of special castes. Except for cotton spinning and basketry, which are done by women, just about every skilled non-agricultural task is performed by people who belong to these castes. The major castes are the smiths (*tumtu*), the potters and handy men (*fuga*), the tanners (*fak'i*), the weavers (*semmano*), the beehive makers and bee keepers (*gagurtu*), and the hunters and foragers (*watta*). Besides these major castes, there are castes of wood and horn workers, civet cat hunters, and magicians.

These castes are all endogamous. Their members are thought of as ritually impure, were-hyenas, bearers of the evil-eye, and eaters of impure meat. In the time of the monarchy they were not allowed to give testimony in court, and were under their own headmen—appointees of the king. Most of them are either Galla or representatives of similar castes from neighboring areas such as Kafa, Janjero, or Gurage. They en-

6 Plowden, 1868: 151–54.

gage in agriculture and their homesteads are just like those of their non-artisan neighbors. Although several artisans may build their homes near each other, they do not live in separate regions but settle here and there in the ordinary communities.

The development of artisanry in Jimma is at least equal to that in most of the rest of Ethiopia. Years ago iron was mined in several parts of Jimma, and sold to smiths throughout the kingdom and beyond, but at present the smiths get their iron from the remains of scrapped trucks and buses. They make sickles, many kinds of bush-knives, plowshares, spears, swords, mule and horse trappings, adzes, hoes, axes, door fittings, and many other items. The silversmiths used to do especially fine work when producing for the king and the king had a monopoly on the work of the goldsmiths. Now the silversmiths melt down Maria Teresa dollars and make silver wire for filigree work; they also cast bracelets, make tiny beads, and hammer sheets of silver. The weavers, today, make plain white shawls which are worn by men and women alike, but in the old days they also wove colored cloth. Jimma artisans have for some time known the use of the rope-turned lathe, and these lathes are used by the wood turners and men who make cups out of cattle or buffalo horns.

Markets and trade

The northern Galla, like many of the highland Ethiopian peoples, are great market-goers, and market activity is a daily affair in each region. Jimma has long been a center of both local and long-distance marketing and trade. The market pattern, which is repeated at several levels of complexity and size, is essentially the same cyclical market pattern found throughout much of Northwest, Northeast, West and Central Africa.

Jimma markets are not necessarily found in towns although small towns sometimes grow up along caravan routes at the sites of important markets. Most market places are simply open fields which serve to accommodate from two hundred to several thousand people. Such markets are found at crossroads, on the outskirts of small hamlets, and near the compounds of important men. (The market sites seem to pre-date the caravan routes.)

As a rule no single market place is used more than one day a week, each one having its own special day. These market days are staggered so that there will be no conflict within a region. The whole countryside is connected by this web of markets and on each day of the week a person in any spot in the country can walk to some market. Similarly, market days along caravan routes are so coordinated that long-distance merchants can attend different markets on almost every day of their march. Merchants going from Jiren to Anderača in Kafa could stop at the Sunday market in Sak'a, the Monday market in Sombo, the Tuesday market in Šĕbe. On their return from Kafa they once again stopped at Šĕbe on Tuesday, at Ule Wak'a on Wednesday, and arrived in Hirmata for the great Thursday market.[7] Each market site becomes associated with its particular day, and rarely are there changes in these associations. Although the fortunes of various markets have waxed and waned over the past eighty years, the days on which they meet are the same today as in 1880.

A small local market may draw no more than two hundred people. At such markets most of the buyers and sellers are women—the wives of farmers, of artisans, and a few women entrepreneurs. Farmers' wives bring small amounts of grain (often for seed), legumes, ensete dough, butter and other milk products, and other foods. Women potters bring pots and round baking trays. Some women make the rounds of the local markets selling the flour of grains they have had ground, or imported curry, ground pepper, flax seed (for medicinal purposes), ginger, or such manufactured goods as soap, pins, matches, razor blades, and beads. A few men attend the small markets bringing onions, potatoes, garlic, lentils, and chickpeas.

7 Cerulli, 1932: 84.

A good example of a major market is the Sunday market at Sĕrbo. Although this market attracts three to five thousand people, it is simply a large open field along the Addis Ababa–Jiren road. On the other days of the week it remains empty. Each type of product is sold in its own area. There are sections for smiths, tanners, women selling baskets or cotton thread, professional traders with luxury items such as fancy knives, flywhisks, silver jewelry, and the other professionals selling pots and pans, scrap iron, and metal containers. Men with large amounts of grain occupy one area; those with lentils, peas, and beans another; those with potatoes, garlic, and onions a third. There are separate sections for the sale of coffee, hides, butter, salt, tobacco, clothing, cotton, firewood, and root crops. And in Sĕrbo there is also a livestock market, separated from the produce market, where farmers and professional traders come to buy and sell. Some men act as brokers and get commissions from each of the parties to any deal they help conclude. Religious pilgrims stop at markets along their route to sell incense, kohl (antimony), medicinal and cosmetic preparations, and such easily carried items as buttons, needles and matches.

Larger markets attract more men and more professional traders, for they offer a greater variety of products and a greater number of prospective consumers. Some petty traders work in small circles following the daily markets, but others travel with donkeys or mule caravans (or sometimes on trucks, today) to neighboring provinces, to far southwestern Ethiopia and even as far as Eritrea and the Sudan.

The market at Hirmata, the trade center associated with the Jimma capital and located about six miles from the palace, is (and long has been) the greatest market in all of southwestern Ethiopia. On a good day in the dry season it attracts up to thirty thousand people.[8] Traversi observed of Hirmata in 1888,

8 Great Britain, 1922: 508.

"Without counting the merchants of the Amharic realms or who come from there, there come together at Jimma those of Gera, Gomma, Limmu, Guma, Kafa, Konta, Kullo, Walamo, Tambaro, Kabenna, and of so many other countries that it would be too long to cite [them]."[9] From the south came lion and monkey skins, elephant tusks, buffalo hides and horns, and some gold. Grühl reckoned the value of the hides, skins, coffee, and ivory in one two-hundred-mule caravan going from the Sudan border through Jimma (in 1925) as £2500.[10] In addition to providing a major outlet for the goods of merchants traveling on the north–south and east–west trade routes, Jimma itself produced a great deal of coffee, cotton, civet musk, hides, and grain. Hirmata was also the greatest slave-trading center in southern Ethiopia.

Some of the long-distance trading in Jimma has long been run by Indians, Arabs, and occasionally, Greeks. These entrepreneurs set up compounds in Hirmata and collect coffee, hides, and so on, until caravans (or trucks) arrive with textiles, manufactured items, and salt from the north. There are, however, a number of Jimma Galla merchants who operate in the same manner. And Jimma Galla, along with men from Wollo, Gondar, Gojam, and Tigre, carry on most of the actual traveling, selling, and buying.

All of Jimma's markets follow the same general principles, though the major centers are more complex. Local products are collected and brought to progressively larger centers, and are finally taken by caravans to the outside world. Manufactured products from foreign areas follow the opposite course into the Jimma countryside. Through the medium of these widespread cyclical, dispersed markets, the inhabitants of Jimma, who do not live in towns or urban clusters, are connected to Arabia, the Sudan, India, Europe, and the specialists of other regions of Ethiopia.

9 Traversi, 1888: 909.
10 Grühl, 1932: 211.

Family, kinship, and community

The basic unit of Jimma society is the patri-potestal and (ideally) patrilocal joint family. The homestead (*k'he*) consists of one or two adjacent compounds, inhabited by three generations: the senior male and his wife (wives); some or all of his sons; unmarried daughters; and some grandchildren. In addition, servants (and, in former times, slaves) occupy the same compound, or even the same houses.

While the father of a family is alive, and while his sons live in or near his compound, he is the final authority in all matters. When he dies his sons divide the old family and each son becomes the head of his own joint family. (There are indications that among the non-Muslim Galla of other regions the eldest son inherited all the property of the father that had not been distributed earlier, and became the authority over the brothers that did not move away. In Jimma, however, all the sons inherit land equally, in theory, and several brothers may live side by side, with each the master of his own homestead.) It is not uncommon for some of a man's sons to move away after marriage. Brothers may move independently of each other, in search of new farmsteads or fortune.

The individual extended family with its male leader is largely independent, recognizing no higher kin-derived authority, and tied to no particular locality by blood relationship.[11]

11 G. P. Murdock has suggested that there is a correlation between the system of kinship terminology he calls "Eskimoan" (1947: 223–28) and societies which place little importance on descent as a basis for social relations. This is the case in Jimma. That Jimma (and most Galla) kinship terminology represents a modified "Eskimoan" type seems to support the contention that the Galla are relatively unconcerned with descent group affiliation in social life.

In the first ascending generation the terms are lineal, except for FaBr (*wosila*) and MoBr (*esuma*), which are terminologically distinguished from Fa and from each other (bifurcate collateral). This may be a reflection of the different relations between ego and these two "uncles." FaBr may inherit ego's mother on the death of the father. (Levirate, *d'ala,* is preferential rather than obligatory.) In direct address the FaBr is called *obbo,* "older brother." Paulitschke

Extended kinship groups

The Jimma Galla recognize that agnatic kinsmen compose a group vis-à-vis other such groups. These exogamous patrilineal kin groups are known as *sĕnyi*.[12] This is a Galla word which has the primary meaning "seed" but which may also be used to mean "people, nation, race, tribe; genus, kind . . . type; relations"[13] In Jimma this word is used to denote any group of people said to have genetic relationship, that is, the descendants of any man, one who lived hundreds of years before or one who died last year. In fact, groups such as Badi, Diggo, and Lalo, which were once independent political territorial units composed of different sibs, have come to be considered *sĕnyi,* and their dispersed members recognize a historical relationship through the fiction of common ancestry. The eponyms of the sibs are the sons of men called Badi, Diggo, etc. Smaller sibs are formed from the descendants of immigrant merchants (*nĕgade*) from the north.

Although genealogical connections among close kinsmen are known, no attempt is made to trace actual relationship within the wider kin group. Each man can recite his lineal ancestors back to the *sĕnyi* founder, but these genealogies are clearly false after the first four or six progenitors. Since these groups

---

translates this word as "Herr" (1888: 288). Perhaps this reflects the fact that among the Galla the eldest brother and the FaBr are potential authorities.

The cousin terminology is also modified "Eskimoan." All the cousins (FaSiSo and Da, MoBrSo and Da, MoSiSo and Da) except the FaBrSo and Da are called *durbi,* "cousin." The FaBrSo and Da are called *obolesa* and *oboleti,* "brother" and "sister." It seems likely that this distinction is based on the potential familial relations between ego and his FaBr (resulting from the levirate), rather than on the presence of unilinear kin groups. The terms *obolesa* and *oboleti* are extended only to the actual FaBrSo and Da, and not to fellow descent group members.

Marriage between any cousins, cross or parallel, is strictly forbidden. Indeed, if the parents of a boy and girl can trace any common ancestors on either side, they cannot contract a marriage between them.

12 Which I shall designate as "sibs," following Murdock, 1949: 47.
13 Foot, 1913: 49.

are not internally ranked there is no value in any special genealogical position within them. People of non-Galla origin may become attached to *sĕnyi,* and so may freed slaves and their descendants.

Functions of the sĕnyi. The *sĕnyi* are not localized, they own no common land or other property, have no joint ritual or religious ceremonies, do not meet together as a whole and are not the basis for most political action. But they are called upon from time to time to fulfill one major function: the exaction of revenge in cases of murder. The pre-kingdom Galla settled matters of murder and revenge, if possible, in the *gada* councils, with the *abba boku* presiding. At these meetings the kinsmen of the murderer and the victim played a role in the negotiations. Ideally the murderer's family paid compensation in cattle to the family of the victim. If, however, the murderer was a chronic offender, or if two families were on bad terms, the death of the murderer might be insisted upon.

During the time of the Jimma kingdom, the kinsmen of a murdered man were called upon to help enforce reconciliation and the payment of compensation or the punishment of the killer. The king held the final decision as to whether or not a murderer could be executed, but the family had the option of insisting on his death, or accepting the payment of blood wealth (*guma*) and partaking in a reconciliation ceremony (*arara*). The members of the victim's family could aid in the capture of the murderer, and if the king passed the death sentence upon him, they could (in the days before rifles were used in executions) actually carry out the sentence under the direction of the king's officers. Conversely, a man's *sĕnyi* was supposed to help him pay blood wealth if he were found guilty of murder. (Peristiany describes a similar situation among the Kipsikis, who also have dispersed and otherwise unimportant sibs.)[14]

Only on the occasion of murder was there clear-cut involvement of the kin group as against all other non-governmental

14 Peristiany, 1939: 121.

Women on their way to a wedding, near Jiren

A Shoan Galla warrior

Jimma farmer and his sons

Young Jimma girls

Weekly market in Gomma

Shoan Galla warriors on parade, in Addis Ababa

A young Shoan warrior

Compounds near Jiren,
with remnants of the palace in the background

institutions. In theory, the *sĕnyi,* like the Kipsikis *kot-ap-chi,*[15] will aid a member if he has had some misfortune, such as the loss of his house by fire, or of caravan animals and trading capital by theft; and it is said that sib members may assemble to rebuke an erring kinsman. But these functions are also performed by the local community, which may bring pressure to bear on a recalcitrant neighbor, or aid one in need. The local community and the kin group thus cross-cut each other, and both operate only through the unanimity of their members regarding the punishment of an offender. The major sanction of the *sĕnyi* is the threat of withdrawal of its support in case of murder or misfortune. The local community has more sanctions affecting a man's daily life.

The official who directed the procedure in murder cases was known as the *abba jiga.* He did not derive his position from any particular genealogical position but was elected by the whole *sĕnyi* on the basis of his wisdom, speaking ability, and wealth. He assembled the kinsmen of the murderer or the victim and led discussion about the course of action to follow. He might also represent his group before the court listening to the case.

Neither the title nor the description of the *abba jiga* appears in the literature on Jimma or the other Galla. It is presumed that this office and the functions associated with it were never of the sort which gained political prominence. The *abba jiga* performed one specific task for a group of normally dispersed people, and acted only through the consensus of others. Thus it was not a position that would normally lead to political power in a society such as Jimma. (Since the Amhara have taken over the courts and police in Jimma, the kin groups have lost their function in murder cases and the office of *abba jiga* has lapsed.)

The local community

Settlement pattern in Jimma, as in most of southern

15 Peristiany, 1939: 121.

Ethiopia, presents a strikingly unvaried picture. There are no villages and no towns, but only small homesteads surrounded by fences of euphorbia or other bushes. Here and there these homesteads are closely clustered, but in other areas they are spread out, and settlements may stand all alone on the landscape. Except where a series of shacks have arisen near a major market, or where a great cluster of houses within a compound signifies the presence of a great man, this homestead pattern is not relieved.

Because brothers often live together, and their children do not necessarily move away, it often happens that the members of one compound are closely related to the people in the next compound. A neighborhood may be settled by a group of people many of whom are related to one another by blood ties. However, these kin ties are not of particular importance as the basis for settlement. Any community may very well be composed of people of different kin groups and even of different ethnic origins. Freed slaves from Kafa, the descendants of immigrant Muslim merchants from the north, and Galla settlers from other kingdoms may all be found living side-by-side with representatives of several different Jimma *sĕnyi*.

Because the homesteads spread over the hillsides and valleys they seem to lack organization. There are, however, informal boundaries which serve to demarcate "hamlets," named collections of homesteads. These hamlets are not economically or politically corporate, but they do consist of people who tend to cooperate and interact most frequently in social and economic affairs. Often several hamlets will be further linked (informally) to form "cantons," and these larger groupings—perhaps forty to sixty homesteads—more or less complete the local community. At no stage, however, are boundaries so distinct as to prevent social and economic interaction in any direction.

Local communities are not necessarily congruent with the political boundaries established by the monarchy or the present government. As we shall see, Jimma was divided into provinces and districts which were administered by appointees of the king. These administrative units were created for geopolitical reasons by forces outside of the community, and were not meant to mirror the reality of local social life. Today as in the past a district may include several cantons or it may take two hamlets from one canton and link them to another canton. This does not greatly affect community life. These communities may be on land owned by its residents or on land belonging to great landlords. The landholdings of great men, like the administrative districts, do not follow community lines. Communities are established in good farming areas and are formed without regard to the ultimate ownership of the land or the political divisions established by the government.

There is a great deal of neighborly cooperation within the local community, although little of it involves the whole canton. Most activities draw some outsiders while a local person may choose not to take part. The activity which draws each man of the canton is grave-digging. One man is elected to the post of *abba laga*. It is his duty to see that all the able-bodied men come to dig a grave, and that there is a fair apportionment of labor. In addition, he assigns to different families the task of bringing food to the bereaved family during the fourteen days in which they are in mourning. A funeral may attract men from some distance, but only the men of the community have duties to perform.

Another activity which involves the whole community is the collection of funds to aid a man whose house burns down, although, as we have seen, this function is sometimes performed by the *sĕnyi*. Every family head within the canton is expected to contribute a fixed sum. This collection is initiated and organized by the *abba jarsa*.

In every community there are several elders who command respect and to whom litigants may turn. Each of these men is accorded the unofficial title of *abba jarsa* ("elder"). If an *abba jarsa* is respected or, more accurately, if a judgment which he passes is respected, he may persuade the community to impose simple sanctions on an offender. But none of these men has any automatic authority, tenure, or official jurisdiction over any region. Disputants may choose to go to a particular elder, and ignore another nearer their homes. In practice, these affairs are handled in small open meetings, involving several elders, neighbors, and bystanders. The function of the *abba jarsa* is to try to smooth over community quarrels before they have to be passed on to higher authorities.

Several men from a hamlet or canton band together to graze their cattle collectively. Each day one man takes the whole herd—which might be forty to sixty animals—thus freeing the others to do other work. (Since the areas in which the cattle must graze are heavily cultivated, herding is not entrusted to children, although young boys are often found keeping the herder company.) One man is elected to oversee this activity. This official (*abba ule*) sees to it that each man takes his turn, arrives on time, keeps the cattle out of the planted fields, and does not injure or lose any of the animals.

When a man needs a lot of help for harvesting or plowing, he lets it be known that he will give a *dĕbo* (a cooperative work party). The man whose fields are being worked on is expected to provide beer and roasted parched grains (maize, barley, or rye) for all his helpers. Such an affair may draw from twenty to sixty men and generally lasts half a day. Those who come are not necessarily drawn from either the kinsmen or the immediate neighborhood of the *abba dĕbo*, and attendance is not closely determined. His next-door neighbors may not attend, while other men may come from some distance away. Much of the heavy labor of plowing and harvesting is accomplished through this community cooperation. A man may pay a debt or fulfill a social obligation (to his father-in-law, for example) by gathering a group of his friends for a *dĕbo*. If he needs just a few extra hands he can enter into contractual agreements (*dado*) with a few other men who also need just a little extra help. A man without a team of oxen may contract to plow another's land for one day in return for the use of the oxen on his own land. These forms of coordinated and cooperative activity are initiated by individuals in their own interests. They are not organized by formal leaders, political officials, or kin groups. Kinsmen do not owe each other much in the way of mutual aid, and individual choice and economic need determine the composition of groups that work together.

Another economic activity involving community interaction is the distribution of the meat from a butchered animal. Except for sacrifices or feasts, cattle are rarely slaughtered. When, however, a man wishes to get rid of a troublesome bull or finds some other reason to kill an animal, he seeks neighbors willing to buy shares of the meat. The animal will be killed only if the owner can, in advance, find men willing to buy enough shares to repay him for the cost of the animal. Anyone, regardless of location or kinship affiliation, is welcome to buy a share.

Religious activity also attracts people on the basis of mutual interest and friendship. The possession ceremonies which most women go through each year, or the celebration of a Muslim holiday (such as *mĕ'ĕraj*, the ascent of Muhammad to heaven) will be held in someone's house and attended by anyone in the area who is so inclined. A house may be packed with thirty to fifty men, women, and children for such an occasion.

Politics on the community level

The *gada* system no longer exists in Jimma. Neither its rituals and statuses nor its organization of leadership have survived the hundred years of the monarchy. Even old men in Jimma are largely unaware of what *gada* was and do not associate it with political leadership and warfare. Some of them do know, rather vaguely, that it had something to do with circumcision and cycles of festivals held every eight and every forty years. They seem not to associate it with the assembly meetings which continued to be convened throughout the nineteenth century.

In the Jimma Galla community there are (and were) no strong leadership or authority positions. There are no chiefs or headmen associated with descent groups or villages. No men derive the right to local office on a hereditary basis and those that are elected or unofficially stand out as elders have positions of slight political importance. If the *abba jarsa* cannot successfully mediate differences between people they have no coercive power to call upon. Other activities are led by elected functionally specific officials such as the *abba ule* and *abba laga,* and these activities are hardly stepping stones to political importance. Thus the king had no competitors to concern him at this level of Jimma social organization.

Slavery

In Jimma, as in much of Ethiopia, the owning, buying, and trading of slaves was widespread. The trade was carried on openly until late in the reign of Menelik II, and Hirmata was the major slave market in the southwest. The trade continued *sub rosa,* and slave-ownership openly, until the 1930's, when Haile Selassie and the Italians managed to abolish slavery.

Jimma's slaves came from a number of ethnic backgrounds, and were created in different ways. Some slaves were prisoners of war; others were enslaved as punishment for crimes or for failure to fulfill certain duties to the state. Many slaves were victims of slave raids which were especially common in areas to the southwest of Jimma. Slave traders and raiders brought many slaves from Gimira, Maji, Kafa and Kullo. Slaves were bound during the marches and were often brutally treated. When they arrived at Hirmata some were sold to local people, while others were taken further north. (A number of the traders were men from Jimma.)

Informants estimate that Abba Jifar II had as many as ten thousand slaves; wealthy men owning over one thousand were not rare. Even simple farmers might own one or two slaves. Ownership of slaves released poorer men from farming so that from time to time they could go on trading trips or attend local markets. Generally, however, a farmer worked in the fields along with his male slave, and his wife shared household duties with his female slave.

As Borelli notes,[16] relations between masters and slaves were not necessarily bad. Slaves lived in the houses of their owners unless they were married, in which case they could build their own homes in the same compound. Slave families were not usually broken up, although they could be. Slaves had the (customary) right to own property, and slave children might inherit what their parents had managed to accumulate. A well-treated slave of a common man could work his own garden, sell its produce, and use the profits for himself and his family. If the slave of a rich man or the king was chosen as an aid and particularly favored, he could become rich and powerful and own his own slaves. In fact, the term *soresa* applied equally to a free man or a slave possessed of wealth and importance.

The lot of slaves was not ideal, however. They had no official rights to justice or to property, could be beaten at will, and could not take a master to court. A slave who had attempted to run away was generally beaten and kept in chains. The common slave's primary hope for justice lay in impressing public opinion in his community—perhaps through the *abba jarsa.* A powerful slave, of course, depended upon his standing with other great men and with the king.

16 Borelli, 1890: 289.

IV

The monarchy

The palace

The heart of the kingdom of Jimma Abba Jifar, the center from which orders radiated to the boundaries and to which great wealth flowed, was the main palace (*masera*) of the king, situated in Jiren. Indeed, Jiren was little more than the palace of the king, even though not all of it was encompassed within the palace fence.

At its height Jiren contained a population numbered in the thousands. It cannot be considered a city, however, in the sense in which that term is applied to urban centers in the Near East, for example.[1] It was, rather, the overgrown homestead of the king, the extension of his household. It existed only to serve the king. Jiren itself was not a center of trade, nor of

1 See Weber, 1962: 71–73.

occupational specialists servicing a hinterland. It did not contain a permanent, settled population; nor did it form a "community"[2] because its personnel and organization did not represent a repeatable form or unit of the society, but a unique institution catering to the monarch.

Like most Ethiopians, the Galla do not build cities as a form of settlement.[3] Their marketing and distribution are taken care of in the hinterland through their system of cyclical markets and caravan routes. Crafts and other non-agricultural occupations are carried on at the local level through the medium of castes of specialists who farm and live in communities all over the countryside. When, as sometimes happens, a large settlement of people grows up around the home of a great man, these settlements are not permanent. They have no boundaries or sanctity and upon the decline of the great man the settlement disappears. The British army's *Handbook of Abyssinia* notes: "The site of Challa, the old capital of Jimma, is now covered with cultivation, and nothing remains of the town."[4] Such is the fate of Jiren, shrunken today to a settlement of a few hundred people who run some shops, bars, and brothels, catering primarily to the small markets there. Most of the houses of the palace and Jiren have been plowed under, and fields are planted where Borelli, Traversi, Grühl, and Cerulli saw royal stables or the compounds of palace officials.

Jiren is located at the top of a high hill. The palace was a compound at least a kilometer in diameter, surrounded by a seven- or eight-foot high fence woven of split bamboo.[5] At its

2 As defined by Arensberg, 1961: 248–50.
3 Addis Ababa was founded as a permanent capital in the 1880's. Aksum and Gondar, the two earlier fixed capitals, evidently never existed as more than the seats of the monarchs and both were largely abandoned after their political functions ceased. The movable tent cities of the kings were laid out as military encampments. Indeed, when the first steps toward the foundation of Addis Ababa were taken eighty years ago it "was essentially a military town and was established on almost exactly the same pattern as the traditional army camp" (Pankhurst, 1961b: 105).
4 Great Britain, 1922: 283.
5 Traversi, 1888: 904; Borelli, 1890: 285.

gate was a high tower, upon which stood guards; armed soldiers swarmed around the front of the gate.[6] Within the outer fence were several more bamboo fences, the door through each guarded by eunuchs in guardhouses.[7]

According to Borelli, the outer enclosure was occupied by the soldiers who resided at the palace; the second was partly for guests of the king. The three other major courtyards were primarily for the king and the personnel of the royal house. At the center was the complex of houses of the king and court, of which the most important were the reception hall (*aderaš* or *golge*), the court (*čilot*), the dining halls, and the homes of the wives of the king. Borelli reports that great houses for feasts were 80 to 100 meters in circumference.[8] Traversi says of the reception hall: "Nobles, relatives of the king, familiars of the court, soldiers, ambassadors, etc., etc., are encountered in this place . . ."[9]

Within the palace lived people who served some of the political, economic, and personal needs of the king and his family. Among these were hundreds of free servants, eunuchs, slaves, and concubines; over two thousand military men; artisans of all kinds; jailers; overseers; and organizers. Near the palace lived court interpreters, lawyers, and musicians and other entertainers. Among the buildings within the palace were granaries by the hundreds, great stables, a place for keeping civet cats (for their valuable musk), storehouses, workshops for artisans, and houses for visitors, servants, soldiers, and family. There were jail houses, treasuries, and a mosque. Traversi gives the following picture of the palace: "Women with skin clothes and with enormous miter-like heads of hair [wigs] or turbans, slaves from all the countries, lords on horseback with wickerwork parasols, mules, mobs of eunuchs, men that labor,

6 Grühl, 1938.
7 Traversi, 1888: 914.
8 Borelli, 1890: 286.
9 Traversi, 1888: 915.

others that drag enormous pieces of wood, aiding the difficult business by singing, give life to Jiren."[10]

The palace had its own administration. At its head was an officer known as the *azaži,* an Amharic term meaning "the orderer." His function was that of a major-domo. He was concerned solely with domestic palace affairs and did not fill other political or administrative jobs. He could order the soldiers who lived in the palace to repair or build houses and fences, and keep the grounds clean. He kept one of several treasuries and dispensed money for certain palace expenses. There were other officers in charge of the labor of the artisans, the care of the palace guests, and so on.[11]

The responsibility for feeding all the people who lived within the palace rested with the wife with whom the king was staying at the moment. (Abba Jifar II divided his time so as to be with each wife for two days.) A supply of animals and grain from her lands was kept on hand by her slaves, and when her turn came, her chief slaves (honored slaves who might hold other positions as well) supervised the slaughtering of the animals and the preparation of the food. In the evening the king ate with the wife of the day in relative seclusion, and often called in musicians (or sometimes an Arab merchant with a gramophone). At noon he ate in the company of his followers, officials, and guests, in the *mana sank'a,* the "house of the table." This great hall had a number of large round wooden tables. At the main table sat the king and twenty to thirty others. The other tables were ranked in importance by their proximity to the king.

The king's servants included many cup- and plate-bearers,

10 Traversi, 1888: 908.
11 An example of a palace official was Abba Goddu Saděčča. Abba Goddu, a slave of Abba Jifar II, was the chief criminal investigator. He questioned accused men when they came to the palace for trial. He also served as one of the chief jailers—overseeing the feeding of prisoners—and was in charge of the treasury in which honey (which came as a tax) was collected.

each one responsible for just one utensil. These and many other palace servants served on a rotating basis, coming to the palace to work one week out of four. Each week another cupbearer came to take over his duties, so that each position had four permanent holders. This principle was followed throughout the administration of the palace, the military, and the police, and was called *kurni.* The free servants who did these jobs for the king were given presents and were exempt from taxes and corvée labor.

Just outside the palace fence dwelt several of the most important palace officials, including the prime minister, the chief judge, the chief generals, and the war minister. Many wealthy and important governors and relatives of the king maintained houses in Jiren. Most of the year these were occupied only by slaves, who guarded them while their masters were away.[12] When great men came to see the king they generally did not bring their wives or families. (Thus Jiren was not a typical community in the composition of its population by sex and age.) Men who did not have such town houses stayed in guest houses in the palace.

Jiren—its personnel, its activities, and its buildings—was entirely concentrated on serving the needs of the king and his administration. Normal trade, artisanry, and farming were not commonly found in Jiren. It is not surprising that today, only thirty years after Abba Jifar's death, little of it remains. Several miles from Jiren were two settlements devoted to trade: Hirmata, the seat of the great market, and Mandera-Set'o, a large plain where transient caravans pitched their tents while awaiting market activity. These were under the king's control, but were socially and physically distinct from Jiren and the palace.

There is little about the king's palace that need have been borrowed from Jimma's neighbors. The great similarity between the Jiren palace and the palaces of many other African kings exists because in all of these kingdoms the capital was

12 The kings, in turn, had palaces in Sak'a, Kiftana, Dogoso, and Hereto; these were occupied by kin, slaves, overseers, and servants.

nothing but the household of the wealthiest and most powerful man in the realm. Throughout most of East Africa the typical pattern of settlement is one of dispersed homesteads, in which the individual compound, surrounded by a fence and expandable to admit houses for wives, retainers, and dependents, is the basic unit. The same was true of the capitals of the kings; and just as a son may build his own compound upon starting a family, so each succeeding king could establish his own new capital. (Buganda was a perfect example of this tendency.) From Pharaonic Egypt to Swaziland there seems to have been just this one pattern for building capitals.

The king

The king (*moti*) of Jimma was not a typical African "divine king." He was not a high priest, nor did he stand in any particular relation to spiritual forces, except insofar as he was "Protector of the Faith"—Islam. His person was not sacred or veiled; he could be viewed by all as, for instance, at the noon meal, where there might be hundreds of guests, officials, soldiers, and servants present. For the most part, his life was not hedged about with taboos. When approaching the king, a subject did not prostrate or otherwise humble himself, but simply asked of the king, "Akkam bultŭni?"—"How did you [polite form] pass the night?"

This relatively matter-of-fact attitude toward the king contrasts sharply with that of the Kafa and Abyssinian peoples towards their kings. An element of the supernatural surrounded the Kafa king, who was considered an incarnation of a major spirit. He was normally hidden from his subjects' view, and when he rode outside the palace they hid from his view. Total prostration was required of suppliants, and even his councilors had to appear before him in hides or ensete fiber rather than in cotton clothes.[13] During the Middle Ages the emperor of Abyssinia normally remained behind a curtain in

13 Cecchi, 1885, II: 485, 488, 492.

his court and "when he rode abroad they all looked to the ground, and woe befell any who dared to look him in the face."[14] In contrast to the Jimma Galla, the Amhara demand signs of obeisance and self-abasement, including kissing of the feet of a person of exalted rank.

The king of Jimma maintained no fiction as to kinship with his subjects. He was not considered the "father of his people," nor did he have any special relation to tribal or national ancestors. He was neither the representative of their kin groups nor their priest; he was their ruler. A king might be feared (as was Abba Rebu) or loved (as was Abba Jifar II), depending upon his own character and his relations with his subjects.

It is clear that Jimma borrowed from its neighbors several cultural elements relative to kingship. For instance, Abba Jifar II had himself carried everywhere by two servants, one supporting each arm. It was said that his feet never touched the ground. This practice may have been borrowed from Abyssinia.[15] A gold ring was a primary insigne of the Jimma king, as it was of the Kafa king, and no one else in the kingdom could wear gold jewelry. He possessed and used fine umbrellas of white silk, a well-known symbol of kingship. An insigne of the king which seems to have been directly derived from Jimma's neighbors and which ultimately involves Jimma in the African monarchical complex[16] was the double-bladed spear (*gonfo*) which served as a sign of the king's authority when carried by messengers and ambassadors. There were a number of these *gonfo* at the palace and they were sent with men carrying royal decrees and orders.[17] No one else in the kingdom could own such a spear.

It is said that in the early days of the kingdom the king wore a conical cap (also *gonfo*) of fine wild animal hide. This form of cap was worn by the Kafa people and king, and infor-

14 Pankhurst, 1961b: 123.
15 Irstam, 1944: 85.
16 Irstam, 1944: 91–98; Lindblom, 1934.
17 Franzoj, 1885: 281; Traversi, 1888: 904.

mants say it was common among the people of Jimma as well. The king simply had the finest in the land. With the increasing influence of Islam, this skin cap was replaced by the turban and the skull cap. The king's turban was no different in form from that of any other man's.

While there were some borrowed traits, many of the trappings of kingship were ignored. Such traditional African symbols of kingship as the drum and the stool were absent. The Kafa king, in addition to the gold ring, had an elaborate crown, gold chains around his neck, earrings, a gold and silver staff, and a special drum.[18] These were never adopted.

The Jimma Galla adopted minor stylistic elements of kingship from Kafa and other neighboring kingdoms, but they did not borrow basic traits of kingship found in these kingdoms. Kingship in Jimma remained basically Galla.

Prerogatives of the king

In contrast to many African kings—those of Kafa and Swaziland, for example—the king of Jimma was not the theoretical owner of all the land of Jimma. He was, however, the largest single landowner, and his immediate family owned many great estates, the produce of which was partly at his disposal. Because the Galla have a pattern of individual land ownership which allows for the accumulation of estates by an *abba lafa,* it was easily conceivable to them that the king was simply the greatest *abba lafa* in the land.

Forested or otherwise barren and unclaimed lands were considered to be the king's. Sometimes these lands were given as rewards or grants to favored followers, slaves, or officials. Often, however, the king would allow landless men to clear, farm, and live on them. These settlers became tenants (*k'ubsisa*) of the king. They worked on his fields or paid him rents or did both. The king thus owned both empty land to give as rewards, and great estates with thousands of tenants.

18 Huntingford, 1955: 118.

The economic powers of the king and the organization of the kingdom will be discussed elsewhere, but some of the privileges of the king deserve mention here. He had a claim to the right tusk of any elephant killed in Jimma, and to lion skins, buffalo horns, and hides of animals found in his kingdom. Any man had to get the king's permission to hunt buffalo and elephant in the forested areas bordering the Gibe and Gojeb rivers. The king could use corvée labor to harvest his extensive coffee lands.[19] He collected various fines and court fees and reserved the right to take one-half of all the lost animals found in the kingdom. He could confiscate the property of a man enslaved for a serious crime or for failure to fulfill his duties to the state. Cerulli reports that the king had the power and the right to make slaves of any conquered populations. In the 1880's Jimma conquered a part of Janjero. According to Cerulli, Abba Jifar removed some Janjero to a region in western Jimma, while letting others remain on their lands but at his disposal.[20] (In 1960 we found that some of the people of Santamma, west of Jiren, were said to be, or to be descended from "Janjero slaves of Abba Jifar who have become Galla.")

The royal family

The king was the head of a great extended family. His mother, his brothers and sisters, his wives, children, and in-laws constituted his trusted aids, his supporters, his advisors, and, sometimes, his potential rivals. If they proved faithful to the king, their positions and wealth were great. If they were treacherous they were exiled. They did not have automatic rights to any offices. The king was not politically bound to the members of his own family and descent group. True, the Diggo *sĕnyi* tended to be the wealthiest and most powerful in the kingdom, and the members of the king's family enjoyed distinct social and political advantages, but in keeping with

19 Onneken, 1956: 82.
20 Cerulli, 1932: 77.

the patterns of extended kinship at other social levels in Jimma, the kin group of the king did not operate as a self-conscious political or economic group.

The successor to the throne was chosen by the reigning king from among his legitimate sons. There was no rule of primogeniture.[21] Before his death the king decided upon his heir. He called his major lieutenants—the prime minister, the minister of war, and any others he wished to include—and told them of his decision. Unless these advisors were united in opposition to the choice, the people would be informed of this decision, and the heir would be known to all. In Kafa the king announced his preference to his councilors but not to the public, and the final decision rested with the council after the king's death.[22]

Brothers who were not to inherit the throne were generally given provinces to rule, and remained men of importance and wealth. A brother who presented a threat to the ruling king or heir, however, might be exiled to another kingdom. (One famous example was the exile of the brother of King Abba Rebu.) Jimma was itself a place of exile for nobility from neighboring states.

As Muslims, the kings of Jimma might legitimately marry as many as four wives at one time. They also kept concubines. Very often the wives were women from the royal families of other kingdoms. Thus, Abba Jifar's wives were Queen Limmiti of Limmu, Queen Minjiti of Kafa (Minjo was the name of the Kafa ruling family), Queen Sapertiti from the Sapera family of Limmu. His mother, in turn, was Queen Gumiti—daughter of the king of Guma.[23] His grandmother, the mother of Abba Gommol, was from the Busase line of Kafa. In addition, the sisters and other relatives of the king married royalty from

21 Traversi and informants report that Queen Gumiti, mother of Abba Jifar II, through her personality and her influence, convinced Abba Gommol to make her son, his third born, the heir to the throne (1888: 917).
22 Cecchi, 1885, II: 493.
23 Cerulli, 1932: 74.

other countries. One daughter of Abba Jifar II was betrothed to Lij Yasu, for a brief period emperor of Ethiopia, and Borelli reports negotiations between Abba Jifar II and the king of Walamo for one of the latter's daughters.[24] Other daughters and sisters were married to men of Limmu, Garo, and elsewhere.

The women of the palace—the wives, sisters, and mothers of the kings—were people of importance and influence in propro-tion to their own personalities and their favor with the ruling king. Their positions were not institutionalized as they were in many African states. They held no offices, had no special courts, and depended upon their husband or brother for all they received. Wives were given great estates and cattle herds, which were cared for by stewards (*abba gurmu*), and from which they collected rents and tribute. Thus they had a source of income and could help provide food for the palace and its guests. Sisters of the king usually partook of the wealth of their husbands, many of whom were given lands, slaves, and cattle by their brother-in-law.

The only woman who stands out in the recorded or remembered history of Jimma is Queen Gumiti, the mother of Abba Jifar. A forceful and intelligent woman, she prevailed over her husband, as we have seen, and for some time hers was a strong voice among Abba Jifar's advisors. She is credited, both by Traversi and by informants, with having prevailed upon her son to submit to Menelik, rather than to fight a hopeless war.[25] It is also said that she was responsible for the expansion of coffee-growing in Jimma. Her success was due to her own qualities, not to any powers inherent in her position as queen or queen mother.

In terms of status, the royal family in Jimma occupied the middle ground between two extremes. In some African states the royal relatives had to be given access to vital ruling

24 Borelli, 1890: 299.
25 Traversi, 1888: 916.

positions.[26] In Kafa and among the Baganda and Shilluk, on the other hand, the sons and brothers of the king were denied any part in the state administration and were kept in semi-imprisonment in the royal palace.[27] In neither case was the monarch as free as the king of Jimma to make the personally most advantageous use of his kinsmen.

26 See, for example, M. C. Fallers, 1960: 67, on Busoga.
27 Cerulli, 1932: 190.

V

The officials

Appointment

The governing of Jimma Abba Jifar was accomplished through appointed officials—not through hereditary chiefs or representatives of tribal or descent groups. Below the king were hundreds of officials in a great many categories: governors, market judges, border guards, tax collectors, couriers, military officers, overseers of artisan labor, jailers, palace officials, and many others. Although the jurisdiction of each official was not always tightly defined, the principle was that different officers were required to carry out or oversee different activities. Offices were readily invented, and titles easily coined by combining the word *abba* with a noun descriptive of the office. In some cases Amharic terms were adapted to local needs—*wŭmbŭri, nagadras,* and so on.

Most of these officeholders were appointed by the king, or by his chief lieutenants with his agreement. None of the offices was automatically hereditary, although any office might be passed on to a son, if the king agreed. The king held all rights to appoint, transfer, promote, and demote officials, and he could devise new positions or mark off new districts. Cerulli observes that "the king . . . appoints the *abba k'oros,* chiefs of the districts. He revokes [the appointments], and enlarges or diminishes the territory of each of these trusted lieutenants by regrouping or dividing their zones of authority."[1]

Men who filled official positions were recruited primarily from four categories of subjects: members of the king's family; wealthy men (*soresa*) who caught the eye of the king or whose family had long been close to the royal family; slaves of the king who proved loyal, intelligent, and effective; foreign mercenaries. In principle, appointment to office was based on merit and capability, regardless of background. Every informant questioned on this matter insisted on this point.

The appointment of relatives of the king to high office was by no means automatic. Sons and brothers of the king could be by-passed, exiled, or removed from office. For example, Abba Jifar took away provinces from one of his sons and one of his grandsons when they were found to be guilty of corruption deemed excessive by Jimma standards. Brothers and sons of the kings were likely to be appointed as provincial governors, rather than as ministers. (As a governor, even the brother of the king was only one of sixty men of officially equal rank.)

Affinal relations of the king were often used in governmental posts. At least four brothers-in-law of Abba Jifar, two of them from other kingdoms, were provincial governors. Such men are naturally more dependent upon the ruler than are near consanguineal relatives. But their appointment was difficult in a realm, such as the Swazi, where the king was surrounded by a strong corporate lineage. On page 82 is a ge-

1 Cerulli, 1932: 76.

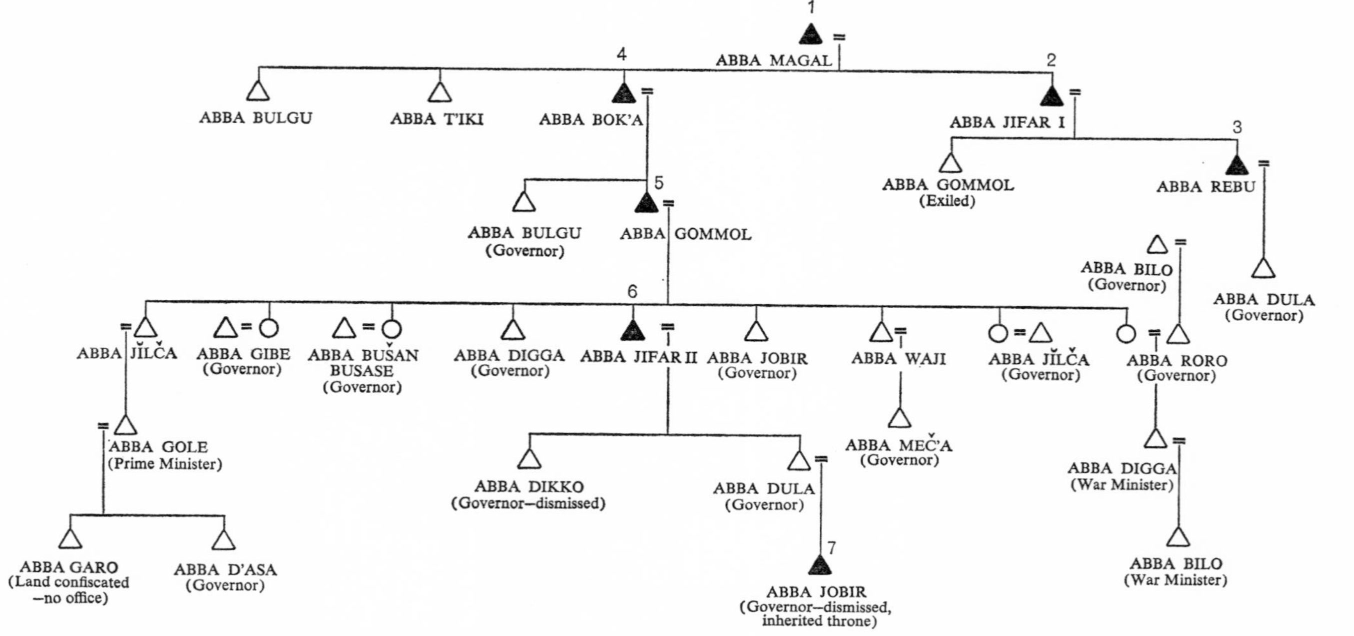

A partial genealogy showing office-holding in the royal family

nealogy of some of the male members of the king's family showing the occurrence of official positions among them.

Although the king was not institutionally constrained to appoint his family and kinsmen to high positions, it was natural that a great many of his followers and closest confidants were drawn from his *sěnyi,* Diggo, which was the group that carried out the conquest of Jimma and made the kingdom possible. The Diggo, in general, had the most land and wealth, and were in the best position to know and aid the king. Otherwise there was no correlation between kin groups and office. This contrasts sharply with Kafa, where clans (if not families) held definite rights to vital positions as district chiefs and the chief of the king's bodyguard.[2]

An example of a prominent Diggo family is that of Abba Bilo of Gŭrrdi. Abba Bilo was a friend, though not a close relative, of the first Abba Jifar, and aided him in his conquests of the eastern frontier. He was still alive at the time of Abba Gommol, and became the first governor of the newly conquered region of Garo. His son, Abba Roro, married a sister of Abba Jifar II (Abba Gommol's daughter) and became the governor of a smaller province in the Garo area.[3] Before the turn of the century, Abba Roro's son, Abba Digga, became Abba Jifar's war minister and one of his closest confidants. He was also governor of Beyyum. After Abba Digga's death in the 1920's his son, Abba Bilo, took over his position, by then primarily ceremonial, as war leader.[4] The relations between the kings of Jimma and the family of Abba Bilo were thus ones of kinship, the *comitatus,* affinity, and friendship. (It is noteworthy that none of the first three men ruled the same province.)

It will be seen from Table 2, listing some officials and their origins, that many confidants of the king, war leaders, judges, and governors were not of the Diggo *sěnyi.* One of Abba Jifar's closest advisors, Abba Bilo-Abba Čŭbsa was of the

2 Cerulli, 1932: 183–84, 189–90.
3 Borelli, 1890: 300.
4 Cerulli, 1932: 67.

Table 2

Origins of Some Officials of Jimma Abba Jifar

From various sĕnyi	
Abba Dula-Abba Jobir (Bilo)	Governor of Mandera-Set'o
Abba Bilo Gŭrrdi (Diggo)	Governor of Garo from time of Abba Jifar I through Abba Gommol
Abba Roro-Abba Bilo (Diggo)	Governor of Nada; son of above
Abba Digga-Abba Roro (Diggo)	War minister and governor of Beyyum; son of above
Abba Bilo-Abba Digga (Diggo)	War minister; son of above
Abba Dima-Abba Garo (Diggo)	Governor of Gŭbŭrŭ
Abba Bušan Gibe (Diggo)	Last prime minister; governor of Saddaro
Abba Dikko Goyta (Diggo)	Governor of Kusaro; son of Abba Jifar II. Removed for corruption
Abba Mĕč'a-Abba Waji (Diggo)	Governor of Dĕdo (part); Abba Jifar's brother's son
Abba Jobir Goyta (Diggo)	Governor of Dĕdo (part); Abba Jifar's brother
Abba Bulgu-Abba Bok'a (Diggo)	Governor of Saraddo; son of King Abba Bok'a. Once exiled to Kafa for some years
Abba Gole-Abba Jīlča (Diggo)	Abba Jifar II's first prime minister; Abba Jifar's brother's son. Very close to king
Sheki Diggo (Diggo)	*K'adi*
Abba Gibe-Abba Mīlki (K'ore)	Governor of Hirmata; Abba Jifar's brother-in-law
Abba Jobir K'ore (K'ore)	Governor of Mana (part)
Abba Garo-Abba Morki (Lalo)	Governor of Bokota
Abba Egan Lalo (Lalo)	Governor of Hirmata (part)
Abba Bilo-Abba Čŭbsa (Sadĕčča)	Governor of Abŭllo. A major advisor of Abba Jifar II
Abba Galan Sadĕčča (Sadĕčča)	War minister; governor of Mana (part)

Table 2: Origins of Some Officials of Jimma Abba Jifar *(Continued)*

From neighboring Galla areas	
Abba Bušan Busase (from Garo)	Governor of Abělti; Abba Jifar's brother-in-law
Abba Gojam Babělla (from Gera)	Governor of Babělla; a leading general and for a while chief of military forces
Abba Jobir-Abba Boso (from Hagalo)	Governor of Jiren
Abba Jīlča-Abba Čŭbsa (from Limmu)	Governor of K'ank'ati; brother-in-law of Abba Jifar II. A major counselor
Immigrants from the north	
Abba Bora Tigri (Tigri *sěnyi)*	Chief of markets and trade; governor of Hirmata
Nagadras Muse (Tigri *sěnyi)*	Chief of markets and trade; emissary to the Shoan court
Kabire (Mantina *sěnyi*)	*K'adi* (first); ambassador to Kafa
Abba Jobir Kabire (Mantina *sěnyi*)	*K'adi;* son of above
Slaves	
Abba Futa-Abba Melre (from Janjero)	Governor of Hereto
Abba Garo Guma (from Guma)	Chief treasurer
Abba Bušan-Abba Saje	Governor
Abba Dikko-Abba Boso	Governor
Abba Goddu Saděčča	Jailer; palace and court official
Abba Bilo Shono	Governor; overseer of king's coffee lands

Saděčča *sěnyi.* Abba Gojam Babělla, a leading general and governor who fought in the wars at the turn of the century, and of whom many legends are told, was from Gera. The king's chief treasurer, Abba Garo Guma, who also watched over the upbringing and behavior of the boys of the royal family, was a slave originally from neighboring Guma.

Immigrant Muslim merchants, or their descendants, were often given important positions, especially those relating to trade or to Islam and its practice. The *k'adis* were often of immigrant origins, as were the men who held the post of *nagadras* (chief of trade and markets). (The *nagadras* was generally also made a governor of a province.)

Abba Jifar made great use of slaves. In addition to the many official functions they performed in the palace, slaves served as jailers, stewards of the king's lands, market judges, and provincial governors. In the time of Borelli, the governor of Hereto province was a slave of the king. This man was from the ruling house of Janjero, and had been captured in war during the time of Abba Gommol. Abba Jifar, feeling he could trust him, made him the governor of a district bordering Janjero.[5]

Some men caught the eye of the king through valor in war; others, especially slaves and traders, won recognition because of their loyalty, special skills, or usefulness. Many regional governors, however, gained their positions through their wealth and their ability to get close to the king. In order to compete with other wealthy men, the *soresa* of the kingdom would bring the king presents and try to spend time at court.

Remuneration

Government officers in Jimma were rewarded in a number of ways, depending upon their origins, needs, and functions. Palace officials were supported directly from the king's storehouses and table. Foreign mercenaries, the chiefs of the tollgates, and perhaps some other officials, were paid salaries.[6] All officials and retainers of the king, with all of their family and slaves, were exempted from taxes and corvée labor duties. And the king frequently, but irregularly, rewarded his followers with gifts of money, land, slaves, livestock, weapons, jewelry, and clothing.[7] No official was allowed to live by direct taxation. (This was in marked contrast to Abyssinia, where

5 Borelli, 1890: 323.
6 Cerulli, 1932: 80.
7 When installed in office, a governor was enjoined by the king to rule well and justly and was given a set of good clothes. Smith reports the same thing in Zaria (Abuja) (1960: 342).

officials were given grants of land over which they had rights of exploitation and taxation.[8])

Ideally, the king did not give regular payment to wealthy men who served him. In the minds of the people of Jimma, the governors and highest ministers were men of wealth who served for honor, power, and the chance of advancement, and to whom the king gave presents and land only "from love." The land which governors and officials owned was not government land, even if granted by the king, but private, inheritable property. These officials may be called (following Weber) "notables"—men of means who can afford to serve without remuneration, who can "live *for* politics without living *from* politics."[9] When the king wished to appoint a poor man or a slave to a high post outside of the palace he would give that man a grant of private land, and thus create a new notable. By creating and using notables the king made an essential separation between private and governmental resources. A man's private land allowed him the wealth and leisure to carry out his functions as a state official.

High officials, especially governors, were, however, in a position to make a profit from their offices. There were opportunities to take bribes, get some free labor, and collect occasional fees or tribute. In this sense the offices themselves were "benefices," although the territory which governors controlled was not. A governor did not live on the rents or taxes from his province, but on the income from his own hereditary land and on the various rewards—many of them *sub rosa*—which he could extract from his office.

The king's ministers

The king had no institutionalized council with fixed membership. There were, however, a number of high officials

8 Pankhurst, 1961b: 124.
9 Weber, 1947: 413–414. In this translation Weber's *honoratioren* is rendered as "amateurs." I prefer to use "notables," following Bendix, 1960: 348.

who were close to the king and who actually did a great deal of executive work for him.

The prime minister (*abba gurmu*)[10] was the king's chief lieutenant. He handled much of the actual business of administration—under the aegis of the king. The prime minister was a close friend and advisor of the king, administered the kingdom in the king's absence, and could use the king's seal when necessary. The first prime minister of Abba Jifar II of whom we have information was Abba Jifar's brother's son, Abba Gole-Abba Jilča. Whatever his fate, he was replaced by an old man (no immediate relative) called Abba Dikko-Abba Bilo. Upon the latter's death Abba Jifar chose two men (neither close relatives), and divided the duties of the office in half. Abba Bušan Gibe was put in charge of the administration (taxation, corvée labor, relations with governors, etc.) of the area north of the Little Gibe River, while Abba Waji Tigre served the same function for the region to the south.

The minister of war (*abba dula*) was another advisor and lieutenant of great power. The most famed occupant of this position, Abba Digga-Abba Roro, held it for many years.

In addition to these men there were two others who, at different times, were recognized as being close confidants of Abba Jifar. The first one, Abba Bilo-Abba Čŭbsa, was a regional governor. He was not of the Diggo *sĕnyi*. The second man, Abba Jilča-Abba Č'ŭbsa, was from neighboring Limmu, and was married to Abba Jifar's sister.

The king was not required to follow the advice of these men, but generally would seek it. That is to say, the relations between the king and his advisors were relatively informal and unstructured. This was a major element supporting the king's despotic control, for a king's council may be one of the strongest limitations on his power. As Beattie notes, councils acted as restraints upon the actions of the kings of such states as Ash-

10 *Abba gurmu* (literally, "father of the shoulder") means "assistant" or "lieutenant." Thus any man from the king to a simple landowner may have an *abba gurmu*.

anti and Swaziland.[11] In Jimma's neighbor, Kafa, the formal council of six great ministers was evidently the power behind the throne.[12] It not only controlled succession and important administrative posts, but could even depose a king for "acts contrary to the laws or the customs of the country . . ."[13]

Provincial organization and administration

Jimma was divided, for administrative purposes, into sixty provinces of unequal size and importance. These provinces were called *k'oro* and each one was under the jurisdiction of a governor called *abba k'oro*. Cerulli writes: "The *k'oro* clearly has a territorial character and comprises a determined zone between delimited borders, independently of the people that live there."[14] These regions were not the equivalent of older political or *sĕnyi* areas, nor of the estates of their governors. They were created by the king for governmental purposes and could be changed in size, subdivided, or merged into others. Major regions, such as Mana, Dĕdo, or Abĕlti, which had earlier political reality, were each divided into four or five smaller units.

Governors were not representatives of the people who lived in their provinces. They did not necessarily have their homes and lands in their districts, although they might. They were appointees of the king, and served where the king wanted them to. Although the position was not necessarily hereditary, the king might permit a governor's son to succeed his father. He might also move him to a different province from that of his father.

Each governor was assisted by a lieutenant (*abba gurmu*). Cynical informants suggest that it was the lieutenant who did

11 Beattie, 1959a.
12 Huntingford, 1955: 119–24.
13 Cecchi, 1885, II: 487–88.
14 Cerulli, 1932: 80.

the work while the governor attended court and otherwise furthered his interests and pleasures. Every province was further divided into from five to ten districts known as *ganda*, each under an *abba ganda*, or district head, who was normally appointed by the governor. The governor directed the lieutenant who relayed orders to the various district heads under him. In order to reach the people in the communities there were a number of heralds or couriers who assisted the district heads. The *abba laga*, as these heralds were called, were also the men who announced deaths in the community, and evidently there was one in each district which constituted a community for burial.

Responsibilities of the provincial governors

The governors were the links between the king and the countryside. They were responsible for seeing that general orders were carried out (that is, those orders and jobs which were not handled by other more specific officers), that there was order and peace within their areas, and that the king was not out of touch with affairs in the countryside.

Governors acted as judges over certain types of disputes. They could not try murder or major cases of violence, but they could handle cases of thievery, disputes over land and other property, and quarrels between people in their districts. Certain cases were handled by market judges, if they occurred at markets. Difficult cases, serious matters, or appeals went to the judges at the palace, over the heads of governors. Of course, many disputes never got to the governors, for they could be handled on the community level or by the district heads. When a mysterious crime was committed, the community would be called together and questioned to ascertain the guilty party. This interrogation, called *k'ore* ("asking"; *afarsata* in Amharic) was conducted jointly by the governor and a judge sent from the palace by the king.

A governor was not allowed to keep a large body of armed men, but so that he could maintain minimal order and keep his status as an important man, a governor could have up to a dozen armed retainers. These men protected the governor, pursued minor law-breakers, helped the governor implement punishment, and acted as jailers. (There were no fixed sentences, but the man was held in the governor's compound for some time—perhaps until he was ransomed.) A governor could not send his men in pursuit of bandits (*šifta*) who preyed on caravans. If robber bands were operating in his area he had to get word to the palace for troops to be sent.

Provincial governors were sometimes responsible for the mobilization of manpower in their regions. One such occasion was for corvée labor (*mŭddo*). Men of Jimma were called upon to plow, plant, weed, and harvest the king's lands. The governors through their assistants, had to produce respectable numbers of men each time they were called for, to work those lands of the king which were within their districts. If a man were caught evading this work he would be fined. His punishment, called *erana,* was to have a work animal (ox, donkey, or mule) taken away from him for work on the king's lands for several months. Men who did other jobs for the king, such as the king's soldiers, the district officers, and the artisans, were exempt from this labor.

Governors were not necessarily military men or great warriors (*jŭgŭna*), though warriors were often governors. In their positions as governors they were not leaders of armed forces, nor could they control such forces. In time of general war, however, they were expected to see that men from their provinces showed up for battle. When the king needed large numbers of men for warfare he would order certain governors to supply them. But, in contrast to Abyssinia or feudal Europe, the governors were not knights or lords contracting to supply military skills and men in return for their positions and lands. They were functionaries who could be ordered to send out messages and mobilize able-bodied men.

A governor could not take general taxation on his own or for his own use. When the king ordered tax collection, however, the governor had certain duties. He had to appoint a representative to collect taxes together with an official from the palace. And he had to send word of the coming collection to the local communities.

The governors had responsibility for the maintenance of public works in their areas. Travelers report that the roads in Jimma were excellent.[15] Roads were large (often twenty-five feet wide), level, and bordered by hedges of euphorbia. Bridges were well made, and some were as much as eighteen feet wide. According to Onneken, men who evaded this work were condemned to slavery.[16]

Privileges of the provincial governors

The governors reaped certain official (and unofficial) benefits. They had the right to demand some corvée labor for their own lands. Bee keepers gave them gifts of honey, and weavers worked for them free of charge if they supplied the thread. Governors were given small fees when lands in their provinces were sold, and they were given one of every two stray animals found in their districts.

Another source of revenue was bribes. A governor took bribes from disputants who came before him in judicial cases and from people seeking exemption from corvée labor and military service. Landowners would pay to have their tenants by-passed when men were collected to work on the king's lands or to go to war. In an attempt to discourage bribery and collusion in tax collection the king adopted the practice, in the twentieth century, of giving the governors 10 per cent of the taxes collected from their provinces.

Although the officers below the governor officially got only the privilege of exemption from corvée labor and taxation, they, too, were able to collect bribes. Every official could find some way to make his office pay. Even the *abba laga* could overlook a man's absence at grave-digging time, or report that a man was too sick to do his corvée service.

15 Montandon, 1913: 87–88; Great Britain, 1922: 300.
16 Onneken, 1956: 85.

VI

Trade, taxation, warfare, and justice

Economic organization

The king of Jimma Abba Jifar directed much of the economic life of the kingdom. There were two major aspects to this control. One was the collection of revenues by which the king added to his own wealth and financed his administration and political operations. Tax revenues were used to maintain the military forces, to pay palace officials, to reward faithful followers, and to enable the king to send elite goods to monarchs in neighboring countries. In the last days of the monarchy much of this went as tribute to Menelik as part of the price of internal autonomy and freedom from occupation by Amhara troops. The other was the administration of marketing, trade, and artisanry in which Abba Jifar and his predecessors played a big role. The kings were the patrons and overseers of the craft specialists, the foreign traders, and the markets.

Marketing and trade

As we saw in Chapter III, trade and markets were of great importance in Jimma, and the market at Hirmata was the hub and emporium of this trade. All Jimma markets were controlled from the palace through the medium of appointed officials. The *nagadras* (from Amharic *něggědě,* "to trade," and *ras,* "chief") was in charge of the regulation of marketing, the collection of tolls, the protection and control of merchants, and the maintenance of order within the major markets. He was a palace official and served as a high judge and treasurer as well. The office of *nagadras* was filled mainly by men who began as traders themselves. They were not usually great landowning nobles in origin, but *něgade* whom the king would raise to high office and power.

A foreign merchant had to get the permission of the king in order to trade in Jimma. A merchant would be presented to the king and give him a present according to his means.[1] Foreign traders who came to the capital and its market had to live —for however long they were to stay—in the large plain between Jiren and Hirmata, called Mandera-Set'o. The *nagadras* was the governor of this district. The merchants were, therefore, removed from the control of local governors and kept under the supervision of the palace.

Merchants were forbidden to buy and own land in Jimma without the king's approval, but they could, with the permission of the *nagadras,* build shops and homes in Hirmata and Mandera-Set'o respectively. Before they could use land, build, or even change the style of a shed, the *nagadras'* permission was necessary.[2] No one could build a house along a road without getting the *nagadras'* consent. Arab, Indian, and Greek traders were required to bring presents to the king before at-

1 Cerulli, 1932: 78.
2 Cerulli, 1932: 78.

tempting new enterprises such as the building of a mill or shop. Other presents were brought simply in order to stay in the king's good graces, and upon the occasion of births in the royal family. In addition, according to Cerulli, these merchants used to pay annual gifts to the king in acknowledgment of his protection.[3]

The *nagadras* in the Hirmata market and the lesser market officials in other markets were in charge of assigning places to merchants to set up their stalls or lay out their goods on the ground. They saw to the preparation and upkeep of drainage ditches to try to limit the flooding caused by the rains. And they were responsible for assigning different sections of the markets to different products, and expanding or contracting these sections as the needs demanded.

All the markets in the land had law-enforcement and judicial authorities called *abba gaba* ("father of the market"), who were appointed by the king and the *nagadras*. (There were two such officials in each of the two largest markets, Hirmata on Thursday and Mandera-Set'o on Saturday.) The men who filled these positions might be *soresa* whom the king wanted to reward, slaves of the king (as was the *abba gaba* in Jiren), or hired mercenaries. Grühl mentions that the chief of the Sak'a market was "an Amhara mercenary in the pay of Abba Jifar."[4]

The *abba gaba* sat in the market on a raised platform, surrounded by a few armed men. It was his job to see that stealing was punished, fights were stopped, and that disputes arising in the market were judged. If a man found a debtor in the market he would haul him before the *abba gaba*. If two men fought over the possession of an animal or other goods they went to see the *abba gaba*. The *abba gaba* could levy fines, have thieves flogged by his men, and order a man to pay his creditor. When one man accused another and they went before a market judge, the loser had to pay a fee to the king. Such fees were held in the *nagadras*' treasury.

3 Cerulli, 1932: 79.
4 Grühl, 1932: 195.

The *nagadras* himself had other duties connected with economic life. He was in charge of the collection of tolls (*k'arat*) from caravans, and of the treasury in which these funds were kept. The frequency and criteria of toll collection varied from time to time, becoming heavier in the twentieth century when Menelik's demands for revenue increased. In general, tolls were levied on the basis of the number of animals in a caravan, and were collected by the border guards (*abba kela*) at the entrances (*kela*) to the kingdom. The chief of the gatekeepers was allowed to keep part of this revenue himself.[5] Once a month men from the palace came to collect the king's share. The *nagadras* then administered this revenue for the king, using it to pay for food for the palace, and to pay the salaries of the *zĕbĕña,* the mercenary bodyguards.[6]

As a judge, the *nagadras* handled cases which dealt with trade, traders, and markets, if they were too difficult for the *abba gaba* or if someone appealed a decision made by a lower judge. In addition, the king might ask him to sit in his place at court in the palace. The *nagadras* became the king's representative in dealing with foreigners coming to Jimma and one, Nagadras Muse, became an important emissary to the court of Shoa.[7]

When Abba Jifar wanted to buy elite goods—such as buffalo hides and horns, lion skins, ivory, colobus monkey skins, and gold—which normally came with traders from the countries to the south and southwest, he had the *nagadras* or his treasurer contact and negotiate with the merchants who brought such goods. These things were given or sent to warriors, visitors, nobles, governors, and rulers of other kingdoms. In 1882 Abba Jifar sent to Menelik the following tribute: 60 horses; 30 mules; 100 large vases of honey; 30 elephant tusks; 60 slaves; 100 sacks of coffee; 20 lion, leopard, and "panther or tiger" skins; 30 horns of civet musk; and some amount (unknown to

5 Cerulli, 1932: 82.
6 Cerulli, 1932: 83.
7 Cerulli, 1932: 78.

Franzoj) of thalers.[8] Borelli describes Abba Jifar's retinue when he delivered the tribute in 1886: "Finally the king comes, mounted on a magnificent mule; at his right is a favorite on a horse. A servant holds a white silk parasol over his head and near him another carries one of green. He is all dressed in white under an ample mantle of black silk. The warriors, also dressed in white, surround him and chant hymns of his praise."[9] Traversi reports that Abba Jifar's retinue numbered four or five thousand people.[10]

Artisans

Artisans, like foreigners, were officially under the protection of the king. Among other restrictions, they were not allowed to speak in court cases. Their duty to the king consisted in donating some of their skills and products to him, in return for which they were exempt from other taxes and duties. The king appointed officers from among the members of these castes to act as their chiefs. These officers were called *abba k'oro*—plus the name of the caste. Thus the *abba k'oro tumtu* was in charge of the smiths, the *abba k'oro fuga* of the potters, and the *abba k'oro semmano* of the weavers. Each chief of an artisan caste had regional representatives (*abba ganda*). The main function performed by these officials was to see that each artisan contributed either his time or his products to the king. The king rewarded these officials from time to time, giving them money, land, or other things of value.

The principal iron mine in the country was in Dak'ano near the Gibe River. (The land was said to belong to the king.) Each year the chief of the iron miners sent smelted iron to the palace as tax and rent. Then the chief of the smiths at the palace had the iron distributed to smiths near Jiren, and they took it home and worked it into tools. About fifty silversmiths and a few goldsmiths lived in the Jiren area in their own quarter.

8 Franzoj, 1885: 288.
9 Borelli, 1890: 159.
10 Traversi, 1888: 901.

Traders coming from Wellega brought silver and gold to the palace, and smiths came to the palace to work on it. The smiths made jewelry, decorated shields, horse trappings and swords. Weavers came to the palace and took away cotton thread which certain of the king's female slaves had spun. (These slaves lived in a house in the palace and had their own overseer. Abba Jifar had brought Amhara women to teach them to do fine spinning.) The weavers returned with cloth and clothing which the king used for his household, kept in his storehouses, and sometimes sent to Addis Ababa along with other tribute. Bee keepers brought honey to the palace. The *debbače* brought civet cats they had caught. The tanners and the men who worked with horn came to the palace for raw materials and returned finished products to the treasuries and storehouses. The *watta* brought water and wood to the palace each day.[11]

The products collected by the king were used to outfit his troops and their horses, dress and adorn the residents of his palace, and reward followers, and they were sent as presents to other monarchs. The king was the center of a network involving the production and collection of various goods and their redistribution elsewhere.

Taxation

There was general taxation in Jimma of all people not exempted for other services to the kingdom. This tax (*busi*) was collected annually and was a great source of revenue to the king. Throughout much of the nineteenth century it was exacted in bars of salt, which were then the most common form of currency in Ethiopia. As Maria-Teresa thalers became more common they were demanded in taxes.[12] Informants said

11 In Kafa a hunter-craftsman caste was organized along very similar lines (Cerulli, 1932: 187).

12 Originally minted in Europe, MT thalers were introduced into Ethiopia as early as the 1780's. Although they are no longer official

that as far back as they could recall the taxation was levied on the basis of property holdings. If a man had both land and cattle he paid five MT thalers. If he had property in several areas he paid for each separately. If he had no property but was a married man or a young man over eighteen or so, he paid only two thalers. A slave with his own house, even a wealthy slave, paid only two thalers. By the turn of the century this property tax was changed to a hut tax. The standard payment was five thalers per household. The head of each extended family paid five thalers regardless of his property qualifications.

In the 1920's much of the tax revenue was sent to Menelik. Cerulli says that the annual tribute to Shoa was MT$87,000 plus MT$15,000 for the army of the empire but Lipsky puts the figure at MT$200,000.[13] To make up for this loss of revenue to Shoa there was "extraordinary tribute, demanded from time to time" which added more revenue to Abba Jifar's treasuries.[14]

The collection of taxes was organized from the palace. Officers of one of the military groups (the *jĕbĕrti*) were chosen to go to the provinces to oversee the census-taking and tax collection. These men (called *daña busi* or *abba fuño*—"tax judge" or "master of the cord") went to the governors of each district where they met representatives of the governor. Together the *abba fuño* and the governors' men went to the various district heads within the province. The first time around they counted the households in each district, putting a knot in a cord (*fuño*) for each one. The results of the census were reported to the palace. After the people had been al-

---

tender, these coins are still in use in certain areas and are worth about US$.60.

The other types of currency prevalent in the more highly developed regions of Ethiopia during the nineteenth century were: bars of salt about one foot long (*amole*), which originated in Eritrea; iron rods; pieces of imported black cloth; and strings of beads.

13 Cerulli, 1932: 83; Lipsky, 1962: 288.

14 Cerulli, 1932: 83.

lowed some time to collect the five thalers, the *abba fuño* returned to the provinces with small troops of soldiers to collect the amount of tax indicated by the census. When the collection from a province had been completed the *abba fuño* and the governor took the money to the palace, where the tax was given to the prime minister(s). The money finally went into the treasury building (Amharic: *gǐmja bet*) where it was guarded by *jĕbĕrti* troops under the treasurer's command.

The governors were not allowed to tax the provinces on their own, and the system of tax collection from the palace was meant to keep them from getting their hands on tax money. In contrast to similar officials around the world, and in neighboring states, the governors in Jimma had little chance to withhold revenue from the king. If a governor was caught taking tax money he was prosecuted. Even after the king instituted the practice of paying the governors 10 per cent of the tax taken from their provinces, the money was not given to them until all the tax from the province had come to the treasury to be counted. Informants believed that a governor got about one to two hundred thalers from the king. This was a good reward, but not enough to permit a man to become independently wealthy.

It is significant that the process of tax collection and the position of the regional governor with respect to taxation was identical in Jimma and Buganda. In Buganda, too, the governor was given a share of the tax revenue only *after* it was brought to the king by specially appointed tax-collectors sent out from the palace.[15] In Abyssinia several decentralized methods of tax collection and remuneration of officials were practiced. In most cases governors could collect all taxes and otherwise exploit the people of their provinces in return for supplying military service. In other cases currency (especially gold) and elite goods were delivered to the king by governors in accordance with the ruler's assessment of their wealth.[16] In

15 M. C. Fallers, 1960: 63.
16 Pankhurst, 1961b: 179–180.

still other cases provinces were "sold" to tax-farmers who paid the king high prices in return for the privilege of exacting and keeping whatever income their districts could produce.[17] The system in Jimma was thus quite different from that of its northern neighbor.

Organization of charity

In addition to the hut tax there was an annual collection of grain and livestock (called *zaka*), part of which was given to the poor and part of which was used to support the religious teachers and leaders who lived in the capital. In theory, a man was taxed on the basis of one measure of grain out of ten, one cow out of twenty-five, and one sheep out of forty. A merchant was expected to give 5 per cent of his wealth. (Obviously there was a great deal of inaccuracy in the declaration of wealth in all of these categories.)

The collection of *zaka* followed the same general principles as that of the regular tax. A representative of the *k'adi* and one from the king went to the province to join a man appointed by the governor. Together they went to the districts, assessed the local people, and had the grain and animals brought to granaries and corrals built for this purpose at the district head's compound. The *k'adi* and the governor were supposed to decide on the local distribution of these animals and grains to the needy. What was left was taken to the palace and distributed among the *shekis* of Jiren and environs. Borelli was struck by the fact that each month the king sent salt to the governors to be distributed to the poor through the district heads.[18]

Military organization

The armed forces of the kingdom were under the direct control of the king and his military leaders. Except for the warriors who lived along the borders of the kingdom and led

17 Pankhurst, 1961b: 124.
18 Borelli, 1890: 338–39.

small bodies of armed men, no governor, *soresa,* or official could keep more than a dozen armed men around him.

From the beginning of the kingdom, say informants, the kings had standing armies at the palace. Abba Jifar I and his successors (until Abba Jifar II) had bodyguards composed of men called *naho moti.* (*Naho* means "follower," "retainer," "soldier.") These *naho* acted as the heart of the war forces and as the king's retinue and bodyguard. They were the men charged with the pursuit of bandits. In most essentials this force seems to have been similar to the military groups of Abba Jifar II. Abba Jifar II, however, instituted a few important changes.

The forces which Abba Jifar II commanded were, in time of war, under one leader, but they consisted of three distinct groups and in peace time were divided among three separate commands. Two of these groups, the *abba k'oro k'awe* ("governor's rifles") and the *jĕbĕrti* were made up of local men who served for only one week out of four and who were repaid with exemption from taxation and corvée service. (The principle of rotation of duties, *kurni,* was noted above with regard to certain palace servants.) Each week about one hundred men from each of four provinces came to the palace. These four hundred men remained for one week, serving under the chief of the *abba k'oro k'awe.* A like number of men came from different provinces and put themselves under the command of the *abba jĕbĕrti.*

Both of these groups had special non-military duties. The *jĕbĕrti* had the job of serving as tax-collectors and as messengers for the king. It was from their numbers that the *daña busi* were chosen. The *abba k'oro k'awe,* when they were not on police or military assignments, worked in the palace grounds building and repairing fences and houses, and keeping the paths and grounds clean. Unless they were called upon for some military or police operation which kept them occupied, these men would return home at the end of a week and new men would replace them. Once back in their provinces they were private civilians and were in no sense available to their local governors as a military force.

The third group was made up of 1,500 mercenaries from such northern regions as Shoa, Wollo, Gojam, and Gondar. This mercenary force was in existence at least as early as the time of Soleillet's visit in 1882.[19] Its members were known as *zĕbĕña,* which is the Amharic term for "watchman" or "guard"; they were paid salaries;[20] they acted as the main palace guards and the king's personal bodyguards and were permanently stationed in or near the palace. When a governor was suspected of permitting bandits to operate within his province, the *zĕbĕña* would be sent to bring him to the palace.

All together, then, Abba Jifar II always had at least 2,000 soldiers at his immediate command. In peacetime they were important for the maintenance of order in the kingdom and they helped the king enforce his wishes in such matters as taxation, corvée labor, and military service. In their function as police they performed executions and were called upon to pursue bands of outlaws which preyed on caravans or settlements.

The king provided some of the equipment for his forces from his treasury and storehouses. Insofar as he was able he supplied his officers and men with guns. (If a man had his own gun and wished to volunteer he would undoubtedly be accepted.) At the time of the visit of Franzoj in 1882 Abba Jifar evidently had only about fifty rifles and a few old pistols. Later he managed to arm his soldiers better. In addition, he supplied officers and favorites with swords, horses, shields, and other goods. The soldiers dressed like other Jimma people, except that (according to Franzoj) the king bestowed fancy "pantaloons" on certain old warriors as military decorations. No one else might wear them "under pain of death."[21]

Each force had its own officers who were appointed by the king. In theory promotions were made on the basis of loyalty and bravery in battle, but the wealthy and important had

19 Soleillet, 1886: 173.

20 Cerulli claims that Abba Jifar II paid a sum to the commander who then paid his troops (1932: 68, 83).

21 Franzoj, 1885: 285, 287.

more chance for advancement. Certain war leaders, such as Abba Gojam Babĕlla, had legendary reputations as great warriors. The higher a man's rank, the more men he commanded in battle, the more booty he collected, the more fame he got, and the closer he sat to the table of the king in the *mana sank'a*. The *zĕbĕña* had their own officers, all northerners. Abba Jifar gave them Abyssinian military titles such as *fitaurari* and *grazmač*. But even these officers were led by the king's minister of war if the king so desired.[22]

It is interesting once again to compare Jimma and Buganda to Kafa and Abyssinia with regard to military organization. In Kafa the "king had no standing army; but he, his councillors, and each of the provincial governors and district chiefs kept a small number of armed retainers . . ."[23] In addition the governors were the military commanders in time of war. In Abyssinia the king maintained a fairly large bodyguard of "household troops," but regional governors had private armies as well. Governors were frequently specifically military commanders who had been granted lands and the right to taxation in return for their military leadership and the use of their soldiers. King Mutesa I of Buganda, on the other hand, "established a permanent military organization, distributed throughout the country under the authority of the commander-in-chief (*Mujasi*). The military officers had their estates in the various districts and yet they were independent of the *ssaza* [provincial] chiefs and directly responsible to *Mujasi* and the *Kabaka* [king]."[24]

Organization of offensive war

Worana or *dula* was an official war between two kingdoms. Formal declarations of war were made, and hostilities begun (and ended), after representatives of both sides met at

22 Cerulli, 1932: 67.
23 Huntingford, 1955: 126.
24 M. C. Fallers, 1960: 64.

the border and sacrificed sheep.[25] The battles which followed might involve both major encounters between large armies and surprise raids on the territory of the enemy.

Informants say that in the days before Abba Jifar II there was general mobilization involving men from many provinces. The governors led groups of men to the palace, where they were put under the command of the king and the *abba dula* (or *abba worana*). The war alarm was sent by the use of signal drums (*gono*) hung in tall trees all over the kingdom. When an able-bodied man heard the *gono* he was supposed to go to the palace. Every man kept a bag of parched grains with his spear so that if called to war he would have food for a few days. If he ran out of food he would have to live off the country, but usually campaigns did not last more than a few days, two weeks at most.

In the time of Abba Jifar II, however, mobilization was less general. The standing units were the basis of the Jimma army, and to these were added as many men from various provinces as the king deemed necessary. Different governors were selected to collect warriors for different battles. In Borelli's time Abba Jifar aided Menelik in maintaining peace in neighboring Limmu, which Menelik's forces had conquered. Borelli was in the province of Abĕlti when Abba Jifar called its governor to assist him in restoring order among warring factions in Limmu. The neighboring governor, however, was not recruited that time.[26]

Decisions regarding war and peace were made by the king and his closest advisors. The *abba dula* was the officer with widest control over all the forces, whether in war or on ceremonial occasions. Below him were the leaders of the *abba k'oro k'awe, jĕbĕrti,* and *zĕbĕña.* The leaders of the specific groups could only order their own troops.

When the king went to war the prime minister(s) remained

25 Cecchi, 1885, II: 322.
26 Borelli, 1890: 322.

at the palace, looked after normal affairs, and protected the palace from attack. Men from the area came to the palace to guard it, and Franzoj says that when Abba Jifar II went off to war it was the old warriors that were left behind.[27]

During a war the king might stay well away from the battle. (Abba Rebu, however, used to lead battles himself.) The warriors and lower officers led the troops into battle—generally in an undisciplined mass. The standing army units were supposed to take the lead. Many men went on horseback and some on foot. (Much Galla warfare during the nineteenth century was on horseback.) A force of five or ten thousand men in battle at one time would not be unusual. Cecchi estimated Jimma's forces in the 1879 war against Gera at more than 20,000 men.[28] Considering the number of men at the palace, those available in the provinces, and the stimulus of desire for booty, there must have been times when much larger forces were assembled. Some men had rifles while others used spears and swords. For defense they had shields of buffalo hide.

Men from Jimma and from the surrounding kingdoms often crossed the borders on surprise raids. These raids (*gadu*) might be ordered by the king, either for gain or for some objective such as the capture of an enemy warrior or the liberation of a captured noble. At other times raids were made by groups of men without the king's expressed consent. If the men were successful they would go to the palace and parade before the king, recount their exploits, exhibit their trophies, and get rewards from the king.[29]

A raid of the latter sort was made most commonly by men who lived on the borders of another kingdom. In 1888 Jimma was at war with Janjero, but according to Borelli most of the fighting was done by way of sporadic raids made by men on the edge of Janjero country. He describes one case in which the governor of Hereto gathered about 2,000 men and led

27 Franzoj, 1885: 287.
28 Cecchi, 1885, II: 530.
29 Borelli, 1890: 347.

them on a surprise raid in pursuit of booty and destruction. The governor had the only rifle (a present from the king) and his men were just a mob with no officers. (In this case the Janjero were not surprised, and the governor's troop was routed. It is interesting that both the governor and many of his men were Janjero themselves, who, belonging to Jimma, made war on their own ex-countrymen and kinsmen.)[30]

In war or after a raid the successful warriors looted the possessions, animals, and harvested crops of their defeated enemies. In addition, prisoners were taken to be held for ransom or to be sold as slaves. Although rich and important captives were generally held for ransom, it was not uncommon for Abba Jifar to invite an eminent captive warrior to remain in Jimma and serve him. Poor prisoners, women, and children, if not ransomed, would be kept or sold as slaves. Thus the fortunes of war could increase a man's station in life considerably, or could reduce him to slavery.

Defense

Jimma Abba Jifar had definite boundaries with its neighbors. The danger of attack from across these borders was constant. As a result there was a rather elaborate system of defense. Where there were no natural boundaries such as forests, mountains, or rivers, deep trenches were dug. These trenches (*bero*) were not unique to Jimma, but were common even among non-monarchical Galla, and among the other non-Galla states of the southwest. They were dug (and renewed) with the use of corvée labor. When the king wanted men to work on the *bero* he sent messengers with double-bladed spears to the important market places of the country to gather workers. Men of all ages were collected and taken to work at various places. Those who were caught trying to escape this labor were enslaved. The *bero* was as much as twenty feet deep and fifteen to twenty feet across. In addition, the dirt from the hole

30 Borelli, 1890: 386–89.

was piled up along the edges. On either side of this ditch the boundary region was a forested no-man's land (*mogga*). Borelli describes the *mogga* between Jimma and Janjero as a wasteland, where people hesitated to settle for fear of imminent attack and destruction.[31] These were often the sites of prearranged battles.

In order to defend the border of the kingdom, Abba Jifar and his predecessors awarded land to men who would serve as border guards. Trusted and resourceful warriors were given positions as governors of the provinces along the boundaries, and the soldiers under their command were rewarded with grants of land from the king. These frontier troops, called *k'oyye,* were to fight off surprise attacks and to spread the alarm through the kingdom. Along these borders were *gono* drums which were beaten to relay the warning to the palace and to neighboring regions. (Each drum had someone assigned to man it.) Other *k'oyye* rushed to the site of the attack to beat back the invaders.

The *abba kela* and his men formed a special type of border guard. Where a caravan route passed across the boundary between Jimma and another country it was necessary to set up a check-point. There were elaborate gates at K'ank'ati, Ančano, Gĕmbe, Danku, and Abĕlti, on the roads to Kafa, Kullo, Gomma, Limmu, and Shoa. Both Franzoj and Traversi say that no one could pass through the *kela* to Jimma without the express order of the king.[32] Traversi says, "A man carried the word of the king to the guards and as a sign presented a lance with two points, a standard that could only have come from the house of the sovereign."[33] Of course, the frontier defense functioned to keep people in as well as out. Soleillet describes leaving Jimma at the K'ank'ati *kela* as follows: "The guards arrived and after having taken the names of the people who wanted to leave they made us jump over the first enclosure. A

31 Borelli, 1890: 323.
32 Franzoj, 1885: 281; Traversi, 1888: 904.
33 Traversi, 1888: 904.

second line of defense is formed by three rows of spiny stakes in the middle of which is built a guardhouse; we came, finally, to a gate and a ditch which we passed over on a drawbridge."[34]

The *abba kela* and his men not only guarded the gates but collected tolls from merchants as well. The *abba kela* retained a portion of this money, and sometimes gave some of it to his men. In addition, the *abba kela's* men were allowed to build homes and cultivate the land around the *kela*. Since these *kela* were usually in depopulated regions such farms were necessary for their support.[35]

The *kela* were guarded day and night. The guards were not used for any other purpose and they were not even allowed to leave their post to go in pursuit of bandits. They, too, had to ask the palace for help if robbers were in their area. According to Traversi, if a gatekeeper let an unauthorized person enter or leave the kingdom, or if he were caught aiding smugglers, he would be sold as a slave.[36]

Conflict resolution and justice

Conflicts were resolved and justice meted out on several different levels and by different institutions and methods depending upon the circumstances under which cases arose. Debt, theft, armed robbery, murder, marital strife, quarrels about inheritance or property, neighborly disputes—all called for arbitration or investigation and punishment. The king was the highest judge in the land and only he could legitimately take life in Jimma, but many lower authorities and courts existed and only a small number of cases came to his attention or that of his chief judges.

The lowest level of adjudication, beyond the immediate

34 Soleillet, 1886: 183.
35 Cerulli, 1932: 82.
36 Traversi, 1888: 904.

family, involved the influence and sanctions of the elders of the community. The state did not intrude on disputes between neighbors that could be settled by the *abba jarsa.* Their sanctions consisted of such forms of punishment as exclusion from participation in cattle-herding pools, funeral benefits, and mutual aid (if the rest of the community was willing to go along with the elders' decisions). Serious crimes such as murder were, of course, matters in which the higher officials interested themselves. But even in the case of a murder the king was more concerned with preserving order than in instituting sanctions. The family of the murdered man could speed justice by aiding in the capture of the murderer but could not punish him without the king's permission. Abba Jifar II usually preferred to have the two families reconciled through the payment of blood money and the ceremony of reconciliation.

Disputes which could not be settled within the hamlet could be taken to the district head, the governor and, finally, to the palace by a process of appeal called *dub'*. The king and the *nagadras* were not the only judges at the palace. One official, the *wŭmbŭri,* had the primary duty of investigating and settling judicial matters. Above him, however, was the prime minister, whose power as court of appeal was second only to that of the king.

Besides the differentiation of judicial officials by level there was some differentiation by the type of dispute involved. This was especially true of the market officials and the religious judge, the *k'adi.* The *abba gaba,* stationed in the markets with their complements of police, acted both to maintain order and to judge disputes centering about such economic matters as debt, property ownership, rights to market privileges, and theft. Cases which were appealed from the court of the *abba gaba* normally went to the *nagadras* rather than to any of the other palace judges.

The *k'adi,* an appointee of the king chosen for his knowledge of the Koran and Muslim law (*sharī'a*), was available to arbitrate questions of marriage, divorce, inheritance, and other domestic and familial matters. He was not given jurisdiction in criminal or political cases even though there might be appropriate Muslim law. This separation of the specifically religious judge administering "holy law" from secular judges dealing with political and criminal matters is very common throughout the Islamic world. "Actual practice severely curtailed the *qâdî's* function. Not only did the early caliphs frequently sit in person, as did even much later governors in the several provinces, but the local authorities, especially the police, arrogated the administration of justice to a considerable extent. In other words, a goodly portion of the *qâdî's* jurisdiction was handed over to the executive arm of the government. . . ."[37] In addition, for many years a council of elders met at Hulle in order to arbitrate domestic disputes according to more traditional Galla custom. This, too, is in keeping with a widespread Islamic tendency, that of allowing local customary law (*'urf* or *'āda*) to exist alongside the executive and religious systems.

Judicial procedures

The procedures for the investigation of crimes, for argument and counsel, and for punishment, were quite well developed, especially at the palace. Certain judicial features were certainly borrowed from Abyssinian models.[38] The Amhara are noted for their high development of, and interest in, litigation, employing jurors, spokesmen-lawyers, character witnesses, judges, and thief-finders. On the other hand, d'Abbadie, Salviac, and others describe elaborate judicial procedures for non-monarchical Galla and some of Jimma's practices may be derived from these older Galla patterns.

When a crime occurred the governor of that area and a representative of the king would bring together all the men of the neighborhood, force them to sit in the sun or rain, and interrogate them until the guilty party was named. If a case reached

37 Von Grunebaum, 1945: 163–64.
38 See Messing, 1957.

the palace, because of its gravity or through appeal, there was an officer in charge of examining the accused. This official questioned witnesses, spokesmen, and the prisoner in a special house set aside for interrogation.

The court in the palace was a separate building. There the interested parties argued and witnesses were called. There was some development of counsel. As in Abyssinia, there were men versed in precedent and law who attended the court, and they might be paid for their services to litigants. These counselors would also be called upon to advise the judges. Such men were known as *hayu* (a term derived from pre-kingdom councils) or *t'ěběk'a,* an Amharic term meaning "protector," "lawyer." In addition, elders and interested parties were admitted as spectators. Speakers spoke in turn, and fines were levied for interruptions.

Punishment for crimes

Franzoj noted that "the death penalty is rarely inflicted in Jimma. It is pronounced and immediately executed only on him who conspires against the king or on him who simply appears to the king to have conspired."[39] Except for recidivist homicide, Abba Jifar II did not often invoke the death penalty. Although the family of a murder victim could insist (to some degree) on the death of the murderer, pressure was generally brought on them to accept recompense in money, animals, or land from the murderer and his family.[40] The amount of compensation depended on the relations between the families involved. The greater the hostility, the higher the price requested.

Franzoj claims that when a murderer was redeemed through the payment of wergild he became the slave of the king.[41] Whether this remained true or not, it is clear that enslavement was a very common form of punishment and one

39 Franzoj, 1885: 288.
40 Traversi, 1888: 912.
41 Franzoj, 1885: 289.

which Abba Jifar II favored. Borelli noted that thieves often became the property of their victims. He witnessed such a case: Two men came in to the king's house (together with a cow to which one of them was chained). One man accused the one with the cow of having stolen it from him. After hearing the argument and testimony, Abba Jifar, convinced of the guilt of the accused, pronounced his judgment, "*Gurguri*"—"Sell him." Thus the accused became the slave of the victim.[42] Slavery and confiscation of property was the punishment for such crimes as banditry, failure to work on the *bero,* to sound the *gono* alarm, to watch the *kela,* or to answer the call to war. And it could be invoked as the penalty for other crimes as well.

There were jails at the palace, and they were guarded by *kurni* troops (about twenty each week) who were commanded by the *abba gǐndo.* The *abba gǐndo* ("father of the stocks") was generally a slave and was a permanent palace official. The jails were used especially, but not solely, for punishing debtors. (The collection of debts was a matter for complicated arbitration and arrangements, including the appointment of guarantors.) Prisoners within the jail-houses had their feet set in heavy wooden logs which served as stocks. Often whole families were sent to prison along with the heads of households. Other punishments which were imposed included the payment of fines both to the victim and to the king, and whipping, which was especially common for thieves caught in the marketplace.

42 Borelli, 1890: 347.

VII

Processes of monarchical control in Jimma

The kingdom of Jimma Abba Jifar was highly centralized, and the kings of Jimma had an impressive record of avoiding the pitfalls of monarchical rule. The regime may, therefore, be called "despotic" or "absolutist." Wittfogel quotes a definition of "absolutism" as "A form of government in which all the powers *must* be vested in the hands of the Ruler, there being *no other concurrent and independent authority*, habitually obeyed by the people as much as he is obeyed, and which lawfully resist him or call him to account."[1] Wittfogel elsewhere notes that the "non-governmental forces aiming at social and political leadership" are "kin groups . . . ; representatives of autonomous religious organizations . . . ; inde-

1 Rangaswami, quoted in Wittfogel, 1957: 103.

pendent or semi-independent leaders of military groups (such as tribal bands, armies of feudal lords); and owners of various forms of property (such as money, land, industrial equipment, and capacity to work)."[2]

Jimma, by these criteria, qualifies as a despotic state. The will of the king was not normally checked by any of the forces mentioned above. Furthermore, neither in the literature nor in the memory of informants is there record of extra-familial rebellion against the king. For example, I have found no account of the king's being forced to send troops against conspiring governors or nobles within Jimma's borders. I do not claim that this state of affairs was permanent, that tendencies to decentralization would not have arisen had the kingdom survived for a longer period, or had Jimma not been checked in its expansion by Abyssinia. On the contrary, comparative evidence suggests that although structural factors tend to determine the character of any king's control, there may be great latitude in the fortunes of the participants in the struggle for political power in any kingdom. At the time for which we have documentation for Jimma, however, the term "despotism" is applicable. This despotism was maintained through a number of institutions, processes, and customs. In the next five sections I shall consider the most important of these.

Recruitment of officials

Abba Jifar II kept a tight rein on administrative officialdom by keeping control over his appointments and by selecting potentially loyal followers. He made careful use of his own blood relatives, by-passing those who were not to be trusted, using those who were. We find him, for instance, choosing high officials from among his in-laws. These were men who owed their positions to their proximity to the king, whose fortunes would fall with his decline. Because many in-laws came from other kingdoms they had no followings of their own in Jimma

2 Wittfogel, 1957: 49.

at the time of their appointments. The monarchs of Jimma were fortunate that their own kinship system forced so few limitations upon them.

Other classes of people who served Abba Jifar as functionaries were slaves, eunuchs, conquered peoples, and foreign mercenaries. All things being equal, such people tended to be more dependent upon the king alone. They owed no loyalty elsewhere in Jimma. Thus Abba Jifar II appointed men who had needed skills, but who were dependent upon or loyal to him. The importance of the mercenary force of 1,500 men, larger than any other force under single command, is obvious. All of these men were alien to Jimma and owed their livelihood to the king. While the employment of mercenaries and slaves is a common technique of rulers, not all monarchs are equally free to make use of such people. The evidence from Jimma seems to bear out L. A. Fallers' contention that "despotism is related to social mobility in that one of the aspects of the despot's arbitrary authority is his ability to grant and withdraw favored positions without regard to persons' status at the time."[3]

Control over the means of administration

Weber writes: "In the case of pure patrimonialism, there is complete separation of the functionary from the means of carrying out his function. But exactly the opposite is true of decentralized patrimonialism."[4] If a king depends upon his vassal's armed forces, or if a regional official is allowed to exploit his province economically, passing on to his ruler only a fixed tribute or what is left over after he has taken his own share, then the vassal or official will be in some degree independent of the king, and the king will lose an important ele-

3 L. A. Fallers, 1959: 12.
4 Weber, 1947: 349.

ment of control. In Jimma the king, himself, was the master of the economic and military means of administration.

The kings of Jimma insisted upon the separation of their administrators from armed forces and from tax revenues. By maintaining a central standing army, by going directly to the lowest freeman for recruitment in case of all-out war, the king circumvented the military potentialities of his landowning subjects and his regional governors. Similarly, the king insisted upon collecting taxes through his own specific officers, rather than permitting provincial administrators to collect them themselves or to levy additional major taxes for their own support. Furthermore, by forbidding governors either to pursue bands of outlaws or to take the life of any of their subjects, the king increased the governors' dependence upon him, and correspondingly decreased the subjects' dependence on their governors.

Several factors seem to have been vital in permitting the king to control the kingdom's economic and military potential so effectively. The recruitment of regional officials was of great importance, especially insofar as the kings made use of *soresa.* Abba Jifar II appointed men whose wealth in land and slaves permitted them the luxury of doing administrative duties without their having to exploit their provinces in order to support themselves. If the king desired to appoint favored slaves or immigrants to posts as governors he simply created new *soresa* by giving them land and slaves.

The *soresa,* although nobles, were not a group whose membership was fixed. The king was constantly creating new ones, and old ones might have their lands expropriated or their fortunes lost through war. Thus the *soresa* did not form a group with a great "solidarity of interest."

In a money economy patrimonial rule is likewise compatible with free transferability of land; indeed new property owners are favored so long as they do not give rise to new social groups capable of acquiring an authority independent of the arbitrary will of the ruler. It is therefore a peculiar characteristic of patrimonialism that it occasionally permits the precipitous rise of a slave or servant to the precarious omnipotence of a royal favorite.[5]

The land and slaves of the ruling *soresa* were strictly separated from governmental resources and manpower. The *yĕbbo* was not a *k'oro* and tenants were not the *soresa's* subjects. The province a man administered was not the same as the land he owned. Nor was a man's land free of control by the local governor or by other government officials.

Following this same principle, the king appointed men to be governors over areas which were not necessarily their home districts. Therefore the governor could be ruling total strangers among whom he had no entrenched support. In no case were governors representatives of local tribal or kinship groups. Governors were dependent upon the king because they did not possess their own "support structures"[6] in the form of loyal subjects or kinsmen; nor could they exploit the people under them for military or economic purposes. The political prize to be won in Jimma was an office, not a fief. Such offices were not hereditary, nor did any man have a right to any office. (Even the heir to the throne was chosen from among several possible candidates.) Therefore there was maximum dependence upon the king.

Another factor leading toward central control of the means of administration was the appointment of functionally specific officials rather than "all-purpose chiefs." In many African states, as in feudal Europe, the men to whom a king delegated authority fulfilled all the functions of a king, though on a smaller scale. They were thus "lesser kings" under a "paramount." "The paramount chief, the subchief, and the sub-subchief differ only in rank: each collects tribute, holds his own court, settles disputes for his own subjects, and performs the whole range of political functions for those dependent on him."[7] Such

5 Bendix, 1960: 365, after Weber.
6 Easton, 1959: 231.
7 Easton, 1959: 242.

an arrangement might lead to a loss of functions by the king himself, and to the secession of a chiefdom or county from the realm of the king.

In Jimma, on the other hand, officials were appointed to specific tasks and areas of jurisdiction. Although lines of authority were not always clearly drawn, a definite governmental division of labor existed. Military, judicial, economic and regional administrative functions were in the hands of different officers, almost all of them appointed from the palace. No official, except possibly the prime minister, was able, by virtue of his office, to handle all forms of governmental activity. The governmental structure formed an organic system, the units of which could not be readily removed from the whole and simply reproduced in isolation. Having established government by ministries the king, as the individual through whom all the ministries were integrated, remained unique and supreme. Competition revolved more profitably around control of the throne than control of any particular region.[8]

Such a governmental division of labor further limited the degree to which subjects depended upon individual superordinates. A regional governor was only one of many masters with a claim to control over a commoner. For different aspects of his life a peasant might come under the rule of the governor, the tax collector, the chief of the *abba k'oro k'awe,* the *nagadras,* or the *k'adi.* Only the king was involved in all activities and each hierarchy culminated with him.

Control of special skills and the disenfranchised

The foreign trader, the smith, the tanner, the immigrant *sheki,* were largely removed from the control of provincial officials, and were under the jurisdiction of men appointed by the king. In case of need they turned to the king. He granted trading rights to the merchant, saw directly to the support of

8 See Gluckman, 1963: 33.

the *imam* and *k'adi,* and gave justice to the artisans. In return he got the benefit of their handiwork, tribute, prayers, and support.

Through control of the work of the artisans, and through the gifts and goods of the merchants, the king received elite goods with which to reward his followers, arm his military, and impress and deal with neighboring kings. By supporting the religious leaders he held a central religious position as "Protector of the Faith." There was no religious force in the kingdom which was independent of the king of Jimma; there were no priests or prophets capable of independent political action. (Muslim saints and semi-Muslim magicians, curers, and mendicants certainly existed, but never seem to have developed any large followings.) The king of Jimma was, thus, an important figure in the religious life of the kingdom.

Other techniques of central control

The extent of geographical jurisdiction by any governor was limited by the fragmentation of Jimma into sixty provinces under approximately equal officials. One-sixtieth part of a kingdom the size of Jimma could not offer a man much of a base for independent power. The multiplication of such governorships (based on administrative efficacy and not on tribal, clan, or lineage boundaries) served to divide the common interest of their incumbents. There was more profit in spying on one's neighbors and gaining the king's favor through carrying tales than in banding together to resist the king.

In addition, the king maintained a number of palaces in various regions of the country. Should his personal presence be necessary as a steadying influence in a particular area he could readily move his court and bodyguard to his palace in that area. Evidently these outlying palaces were used more widely early in the history of Jimma than at later periods. There is evidence that Abba Jifar I spent a great deal of time at the palace in Sak'a (Čalla), the area that had been the capital of the Badi, his chief rivals. In addition, there are references to his having spent part of his time in Dogoso, to the east of Jiren, although Jiren was the center of operations. By the time of Abba Jifar II there was less need for these other palaces, although they were used from time to time.

Communications

The histories of kingdoms and empires in Africa, Europe, and Asia provide ample evidence that administrators and generals at the frontiers of states, facing hostile outsiders, or perhaps simply far from their states' centers of power, are constant threats to central authority.

> The decline of central authority is also furthered by the official's physical distance from the center of authority. Unless a realm is compact, transportation good, and the dependence of the people upon the central authority crucial . . . officials become more independent as their distance from the center increases. . . . They will utilize local resources independently, and difficulties of communication plus the need for quick decisions may increase their autonomy still further.[9]

There is some evidence that Jimma was not totally unaffected by this "law" of monarchical rule. The governors that lived along the borders were, after all, in control of the *k'oyye* who formed the border guard. The operation Borelli describes, in which the governor of a border district gathered one to two thousand men for a raid on Janjero, would have been impossible for a governor of a province not on the border. Independent action of this sort was possible only for an official required to make quick decisions regarding the use of armed men. The very exigencies of border-keeping tend to build up a special position for the officer in charge, transforming him from a subordinate of the king to a leader of men.

That such border governors never *did* succeed (to my knowledge) in becoming dangerously independent seems to be

9 Bendix, 1960: 351.

due to the compactness of the kingdom and the effectiveness of communications within it. From the capital it did not take many hours for horsemen to reach any part of the kingdom. With good roads, no internal geographical barriers, and good horses (more common in the nineteenth century than today) it was possible for the palace to keep a rein on the outlying regions. Had Jimma continued to grow in size, or had its military forces conquered other countries beyond the range of easy transportation, there would be reason to expect an increase in independence on the part of the king's representatives in those areas.

VIII

The origins of monarchy and despotism in Jimma

Jimma compared to its neighbors

In the preceding chapters I suggested that Jimma was quite distinctive in its political structure compared to the non-Galla states surrounding it. I took as particular points of comparison Kafa, the greatest and strongest of Jimma's immediate neighbors, which is said to have occupied the Jimma area before the coming of the Galla, and Abyssinia, the oldest, most powerful state in that part of the world and Jimma's eventual master. If we compare these states with respect to the variables discussed in Chapter I, we find that in each case Jimma is quite different.

(1) System of appointment of officials: The king of Jimma was consistently freer in his power to appoint followers to positions of importance. Both the Abyssinian and Kafa adminis-

trations were partly in the hands of local hereditary dynasties, and in Kafa, at least, clans held prescriptive rights to a great many vital positions. Clearly Abyssinia was much closer to Jimma in this matter than was Kafa. There were periods in history when the emperors of Abyssinia were powerful enough to shift and appoint their officials as they wished. The situation was changing and complex, dependent upon the dynamics of rule in that state. My point is, however, that Jimma was far from a simple copy of Abyssinia in its administrative aspects.

(2) Organization of administrative activity: In Jimma the monarch consistently maintained remarkable control over the functions performed by his followers. In the vital concerns of control over an army and tax collection Jimma shows itself to have been far more centralized than either of its great neighbors. In Jimma, in contrast to the other two, there were no private armies, and there was no independent collection of taxation.

(3) The aura of kingship: Here, too, Jimma differed from Kafa and Abyssinia. Whereas the Kafa king was a fine example of a "divine monarch," and the Abyssinian kings were surrounded by taboos and an element of the sacred, the king of Jimma was considered to be only a powerful mortal. Clearly he was not modeled after the kings of Kafa and Abyssinia.

Little has been said about the neighboring Galla states of Limmu, Gomma, Guma, and Gera. There is not enough evidence available about these monarchies to be able to compare them with Jimma structurally. It is possible to say, on the basis of Cecchi's account primarily, that these kingdoms shared a number of features with Jimma. For example, the kings were not considered sacred personages but they did stand out above any other political figures in these states. In Cerulli's collection of folktales and poetry[1] all the warriors and heroes appear to be directly subservient to the kings. These kingdoms were organized into provinces (*k'oros*) with *abba gandas* below the *abba k'oros*. The official called the *abba mizan* ("father of the

1 Cerulli, 1922.

scales") in Gera seems to have been the same as the *nagadras* in Jimma.[2] All had similar border guards, customs gates, alarm drums, and war organization.[3] In these respects they shared a common political culture with Jimma. The data are not full enough, however, to allow a judgment as to how much these kingdoms resembled Jimma in its despotic and bureaucratic aspects.

Jimma as a bureaucracy

One over-all characteristic of Jimma separates it from its neighbors quite clearly. Jimma comes much closer than the others to approximating the model of a bureaucratic structure as formulated by Max Weber.[4] Although the king attempted to keep his administration tied to himself as an individual, the nature of the administrative structure was relatively impersonal. Men in positions of authority related to each other with reference to the offices they held, not because of their personal qualities, family, or kinship backgrounds. Kinsmen might (and surely did) give each other preference, and nepotism was general, but it did not form the ideal basis of government.

The government was a continuously functioning structure. Office-holders were not appointed on just a case to case basis by the ruler; they had definite duties, and these duties were inherent in the office rather than its occupant. Offices were ranked, and there was a system of supervision and appeal. The ranking system was independent of the personal characteristics of holders of specific offices. Administrative offices were not the personal property of their occupants, to be sold, leased, or bequeathed. Nor were the military and economic resources appropriate to the office the property of the incumbent. The forces of the *abba gaba* and *abba ǧindo* were not their own kinsmen, armies, or followers, but the human resources necessary for the fulfillment of the specific duties of these positions.

2 Cecchi, 1885, II: 166–67.
3 Cecchi, 1885, II: *passim.*
4 Weber, 1947: 329–41; Bendix, 1960: 418–25.

In addition, the use of force by officials was circumscribed and limited (ideally) to certain definite circumstances.

Government in Jimma was government by ministries, not by chiefs. Below the level of prime minister there was a degree of separation of officialdom into the categories of military, economic, judicial, religious, and regional-administrative. The lines often intersected, especially where adjudication was involved, but the division of labor was real, even if rudimentary. There was a relatively high degree of political role differentiation between spheres of activity, between political roles, and between the operations performed at different levels within the system. (These are characteristics which Easton suggests will be found to increase with the level of political complexity.[5]

Jimma bureaucracy was clearly not of a modern type. Record keeping was slight, though Abba Jifar II did have personal scribes and records were taken for taxation purposes. Little training was required for most positions, and there was no system of examination or civil service tenure. Office holders were not "career" officers, and most of them were not "remunerated by fixed salaries in money."[6] In the outline of its structure, however, Jimma does represent a simple bureaucratic form. It is suggested, furthermore, that underlying much of this structure were certain aspects of pre-monarchical Galla socio-political organization.

The legacy of the pre-kingdom organization

Certain characteristics of Jimma government, particularly those that seem most bureaucratic, and conducive to despotism were typical (though in rudimentary form) of the "republican" Galla. Where chiefdoms arose among the Galla some of these tendencies were manifested on a new level of organization.

5 Easton, 1959: 240–41.
6 Weber, 1947: 332.

Galla socio-political organization (like that of the Nandi and other East African peoples) was based on non-ascriptive, non-kinship, "universalistic" principles. Kinship beyond the extended family was not a basis for common economic activity, common residence, or political activity. Nor did the Galla live in villages with traditional headmen. Galla society therefore did not have many traditional leadership positions derived automatically through ascriptive criteria. There was no development of lineage or tribal headmen, no "ramage" organization. L. A. Fallers notes that when such African states as the Zulu and Ashanti moved in the direction of greater centralization these developments "seem typically to have resulted from the efforts of paramount chiefs to lessen their dependence upon the loyalty of lineage heads by building up central administrative staffs . . ."[7] In Jimma the kings never had to contend with lineages having political leaders. There were other consequences of the lack of corporate kin groups. The king himself was not accountable to his own kin group and was therefore unlimited in his appointment of officials by the need to appoint relatives to important posts. The king's power did not rest on his position within a particular clan or tribe. Furthermore, because the ownership of wealth in land and other property was within the individual family, it was possible for the king to expropriate the land of a noble without alienating a large group of kinsmen. Similarly, an official could be removed from office, exiled, or enslaved, without incurring the displeasure of many people. The individual ownership of wealth allowed an administration by use of "notables." There were people in Jimma who were able to rule without remuneration from fiefs, tax-farming, or their own kinsmen-followers.

Leadership in Galla society was charismatic, elective, or based on control derived through individual or extended family wealth. No Galla leaders had the "right" to lead; and no one was necessarily a leader for life. Indeed, the *gada* system decreed that no man might serve for more than eight years. Be-

7 L. A. Fallers, 1963: 321.

fore his grade was in power, and after its term was finished, he was not supposed to serve as leader in war or council. (We have seen that this proscription was sometimes by-passed, but it existed as an ideal.)

Galla leadership was, to some extent, functionally specific. The elected *gada* officials (*abba boku, abba sa'a, abba dula*) were all officers with specific jobs. The *abba boku* led in council; the *abba dula* led in war. (The function of the *abba sa'a* is not clear from the literature.)[8] Even the official who called together *sĕnyi* meetings was essentially an elected leader whose functions were defined and who was removable from office. Galla leaders are (ideally) not "chiefs" and "subchiefs," but "officers." When Gama-Moras (see pp. 31 and 32 above) made himself ruler his first acts of governmental reorganization in Gudru, according to Massaja, were to appoint, not "lieutenants," but a "chief of all his soldiers" and a "judge of the market with authority over caravans, over merchants, and over all that pertains to commerce."[9]

The most important sources of leadership and control seem always to have revolved around warfare and markets. Gama-Moras made his climb to power through both of these activities, but at the beginning of his reign he delegated their control to his subordinates. In the monarchies the king took upon himself and his administration the central leadership functions. Since he did not farm these functions out to nobles, the king shut off one source of competition for leadership. Among the Galla, in addition, there was no continual production of potentially competitive leadership through kinship or village groupings.

Another important characteristic of the western Galla which was vital in Jimma was the free use of foreigners for political and economic functions. The Galla, from the litera-

8 D'Abbadie says that the *abba sa'a* "levies the cattle taxes for the needs of the state" (1880: 176). This could refer to collections for mutual aid.

9 Massaja, 1886, III: 180.

ture, seem to have been quite ready and willing to use, hire, and follow foreigners. Plowden and Bell were held by the Gudru Galla (before the time of Gama-Moras) for a number of months, in order that they might help the Gudru fight over Galla. The Gudru even begged Plowden to remain with them as a leader.[10] The two appointees of Gama-Moras mentioned above were not natives of Gudru, and were probably not even Galla. The controller of the markets was a rich merchant who had lived in Gudru for some years; the man created chief of the armies (who had an Amhara name) was one of Gama-Moras' hired mercenaries, chosen partly for his ability to handle rifles.[11] Harris tells of an Amhara noble who, having been exiled from Shoa, led Galla warriors against his enemies, carrying on campaigns for some years.[12] Cerulli's material contains a number of references to Galla shifting loyalty and working for new masters. One example involves Abba Jifar II: "Asin Said was a native of Gimma Abba Gifar, and husband of Tullu Abba Gifar's sister. He was banished from Gimma and went to Guma, where he became at once famous on account of his Moslem zeal. . . . Abba Čubir [the Guma king] became very partial to him, and gave him great presents."[13] Conversely, Abba Jifar II tried to convince one of his fathers-in-law, a famous warrior and counselor to the queen of Gera, to desert his own country and come to Jimma. When the queen learned of his intention to leave Gera she had him imprisoned and put in stocks. Abba Jifar first tried to ransom him with gold, and finally went to war with Gera over the matter.[14]

As we have seen, Abba Jifar II made use of immigrants and mercenaries of all kinds, all origins. A most important aspect of his control was his ability to hire and use such people. Evidently the "universalistic" Galla have for some time felt free to recruit useful foreigners to their service.

10 Plowden, 1868: 290 ff.
11 Massaja, 1886, III: 180.
12 Harris, 1844: 96–145.
13 Cerulli, 1922: 51.
14 Cecchi, 1885, II: 321.

The king of Jimma inherited his position as patron of the artisans and the foreign traders, and controller of the markets, from his pre-kingdom predecessors. The *abba boku* (or *hayu*) was the official protector of the artisans and strangers. Cerulli noted this among the Gombiču Galla of Shoa, and claims that the *hayu* collected tribute from these people at the ceremony in which the laws relating to their blood wealth were recited. In theory, at least, if he did not decree the amount of compensation to be paid for the death of an artisan or foreigner the murderer would be free from liability.[15] Plowden gives us the following information about the control of merchants in Gudru: "Each man on his father's land is master; the public road even is thus private property, and the merchant may be stopped at the door of every hut, till he makes terms with the proprietor. The limit to this is as follows: each merchant places himself under the protection of some Galla of influence, who pleads and answers for him in every case that may arise."[16] And, as we have seen, market control was a vital aspect of leadership among the western Galla.

The disappearance of gada

Gada has been considered such a vital part of Galla life that its disappearance from Jimma demands an explanation. Even before the foundation of the kingdom its political functions had been weakened by the growth of strong leaders but that so few traces survived to the 1960's indicates that the elements of *gada* were under attack from several directions.

Gada had at least three important functions: (1) it was the basis for an assembly for arbitration, a tribunal; (2) it was the basis for recruitment of leaders and the apportionment of political tasks; (3) it provided a system of age status, of ritual, and of life-crisis rites. It was evidently a long time before *gada* was totally replaced as an assembly of elders, since such meetings continued throughout the nineteenth century, al-

15 Cerulli, 1932, 48–49, 80.
16 Plowden, 1868: 308.

though with restricted jurisdiction and disassociated from the rest of the *gada* system. Those who attended were elders representing families and kin groups rather than all the members of a particular age grade and set, and the system of customary law they represented was decreasing in influence due to the development of both Islamic and executive legal systems. The other political connotations of *gada*, and its leadership patterns, were more directly attacked by the powerful organization of the monarchy with its monopoly of force and its economic power. Landlords, war leaders, kings, governors, and market administrators all undercut these aspects of *gada*.

The other blow to the *gada* system was the adoption of Islam, which meant not only a new god and new spirits but also new festivals, new religious practices, and a new system of rites of passage. Circumcision now had to be done early in life rather than after the fourth grade, as it had been in *gada*. Cattle could no longer be speared for ritual purposes (which had been basic to *gada* ceremonies) but had to have their throats cut and the proper Muslim prayers said. Islam, as the faith of the king and the great men of the kingdom, had high prestige and it soon spread to the whole population. With this replacement of its several functions through new institutions, it is understandable that *gada* has not survived.

The influence of Islam

Islam was probably useful to the early kings, allowing them to break more fully with the traditions of the past and from the rituals and associations of the *gada* system. Islamic thought also gives legitimacy to strong leadership of the secular state. But Jimma had a king before it had Islam and it seems unlikely that the political structure and the despotic condition of Jimma was developed through Muslim influence and models.

Muslim philosophers may have sanctioned strong states and authoritarian caliphs as necessary to protect the community of believers, but this political theory failed to centralize Islamic states. Although at times such dynasties as the late Umayyads and the early 'Abbāsids were successfully centralized, more often "actual government resembles rather closely medieval government elsewhere. . . . The ruler's influence was apt to decline with distance from his residence; in the later period, many a sultan led the migratory life typical of the German emperors."[17] The theory of strong government is not spelled out in the Koran and there are no general and widely known principles or methods through which this ideal strong state is to be established and maintained. The practices of Muslim states were varied and changing and must be reconstructed by historical scholarship. It is not likely that nineteenth-century merchants from northern Ethiopia and the Sudan could have imparted much Muslim political theory to Abba Jifar I and his successors. When Jimma's kings borrowed political institutions they evidently turned to their neighbors, Kafa and Abyssinia. In fact, a number of political institutions in Jimma which parallel institutions of the Baghdad caliphate have Amharic names.[18] Islam cannot, in short, be considered a vital influence on either the origin of Jimma Abba Jifar or the development of its structure.

Conclusions

The political structure of Jimma Abba Jifar was not a simple transferral of a foreign political system to a Galla people. At least three distinct processes contributed to the formation of its characteristic political system.

(1) there was an initial period of interaction among Galla groups and between Galla and non-Galla that led to the de-

17 Von Grunebaum, 1955: 136.
18 For example, in Jimma they use the Amharic-derived *nagadras* instead of the Arabic *muḥtasib,* ("market superintendent"); the Amharic *gĭmja bet* instead of the Arabic *bayt al-māl,* ("treasury"); and the Amharic *wŭmbŭri* instead of the Arabic *wazir,* ("prime minister"). (Of course all of these are so common to monarchies everywhere that their mere presence in both Jimma and Baghdad cannot indicate any necessary relationship.)

velopment of war leaders with administrative staffs and to increasing control over political units.

(2) When creating an administration and founding a regime the Galla political leaders and their people must have turned to existing patterns of organization, the ones they were most familiar with, and re-used and re-worked them in new ways.

(3) Useful concepts, traits, and practices were constantly being borrowed. Others which were inimical to tradition or contrary to the needs of the king or his followers were ignored.

I suggest that whenever the origins of states are considered we must take into account at least these three processes. The origins of Jimma Abba Jifar may be traced to a milieu in which there was continual armed conflict. This warfare led to increased need for coordination and leadership of local groups. (We would expect that the need for organization would have been greatest where the Galla were opposed by forces from strong kingdoms, and, in fact, Galla monarchies developed only in regions bordering on already established kingdoms.) The various conquests of one local group by another, of which we are fortunate to have some documentation, were both important consequences of the stimuli to the intensification of rule by individuals.

In non-monarchical Galla socio-political organization we have noted some of the basic elements of a rational bureaucratic organization: (*a*) the predominance of territoriality, rather than descent, as a basis for group action; (*b*) vertical mobility and the ready recognition of achieved status; (*c*) the appointment of both temporary and functionally specific officers; (*d*) the easy incorporation of foreigners.

This particular combination of historical events and the cultural context in which they occurred may have been unique to Jimma Abba Jifar, but the processes involved are not. They are found repeatedly in different parts of the world, and an awareness of them may aid us in the study of the development of states and the dynamics of monarchical rule.

Bibliography

Abbadie, Antoine d'. 1880. "Sur les Oromo, Grande Nation Africaine," *Annales de la Société Scientifique de Bruxelles,* IV: 167–92.

Abebe Ambatchew and others. 1957. *Field Trip to Nakamte.* Ethnological Society Bulletin, No. 6. Addis Ababa: University College of Addis Ababa.

Albert, E. 1960. "Rwanda vs. Urundi," *Southwestern Journal of Anthropology,* XVI: 46–74.

Arensberg, C. M. 1961. "The Community as Object and as Sample," *American Anthropologist,* LXIII: 241–64.

Asmarom Legesse. 1963. "Class Systems based on Time," *Journal of Ethiopian Studies,* I: 1–29.

Aubry, A. 1887. "Une Mission au Shoa et dans les Pays Gallas," *Bulletin de la Société de Géographie de Paris,* VII–VIII: 439–85.

Azaïs, R. P., and R. Chambard. 1931. *Cinq Années de Recherches Archéologiques en Éthiopie.* Paris: Paul Geuthner.

Baeteman, J. 1929. *Dictionnaire Amarigna-Francais.* Dire Dawa: Saint Lazare.

Barnes, J. A. 1955. *Politics in a Changing Society.* London: Oxford University Press.

Beattie, J. H. M. 1959. "Checks on the Abuse of Political Power in Some African States," *Sociologus,* n.s., IX: 97–115.

———. 1960. *Bunyoro.* New York: Holt, Rinehart and Winston.

———. 1961. "Democratization in Bunyoro," *Civilisations,* X: 8–20.

Beckingham, C. F., and G. W. B. Huntingford. 1954. *Some Records of Ethiopia, 1593–1646.* London: Hakluyt Society.

Beke, C. T. 1843. "On the Countries South of Abyssinia," *Journal of the Royal Geographical Society,* XIII: 254–68.

Bendix, R. 1960. *Max Weber: An Intellectual Portrait.* New York: Doubleday.

Benet, F. 1957. "Explosive Markets: The Berber Highlands," in *Trade and Markets in the Early Empires,* ed. by K. Polanyi, C. M. Arensberg, and H. W. Pearson. Glencoe, Ill.: The Free Press.

Bieber, F. J. 1908. "Das Hochland von Südäthiopien," *Petermann's Geographische Mitteilungen,* LIV: 1–6, 111–13.

———. 1920–23. *Kaffa: Ein Altkuschitisches Volkstum in Inner-Afrika.* Münster: Anthropos-Bibliothek, Vol. I, 1920; Vol. II, 1923.

Bieber, O. 1948. *Geheimnisvolles Kaffa; Im Reich der Kaiser-Götter.* Vienna: Universum Verlagsges.

Bohannan, L. 1958. "Political Aspects of Tiv Social Organization," in *Tribes Without Rulers,* ed. by J. Middleton and D. Tait. London: Routledge and Kegan Paul.

Borelli, J. 1890. *Ethiopie Méridionale.* Paris: Ancienne Maison Quantin.

Bradbury, R. 1957. *The Benin Kingdom.* Ethnographic Survey of Africa. London: International African Institute.

Brooke, Clarke H., Jr. 1957. "A Study of Galla Settlements: Hararge Province, Ethiopia." Unpublished Ph.D. dissertation, University of Nebraska.

Cecchi, A. 1885. *Da Zeila alla Frontiere del Caffa,* 3 vols. Rome: E. Loescher.

Cerulli, Enrico. 1922. *Folk-Literature of the Galla of Southern Ethiopia.* Harvard African Studies, III. Cambridge, Mass.: The Peabody Museum of Harvard University.

———. 1932–33. *Etiopia Occidentale,* 2 vols. Rome: Sindacato Italiano Arti Grafiche.

Cerulli, Ernesta. 1956. *Peoples of South-West Ethiopia and Its Borderland.* Ethnographic Survey of Africa. London: International African Institute.

Colson, E. 1958. "The Role of Bureaucratic Norms in African Political Structures," *Proceedings of the American Ethnological Society,* Annual Spring Meeting: 42–49.

Consociazione Turistica Italiana. 1938. *Guida dell'Africa Orientale Italiana.* Milan: Consociazione Turistica Italiana.

Coulborn, R., ed. 1956. *Feudalism in History.* Princeton, N.J.: Princeton University Press.

Doresse, J. 1959. *Ethiopia.* London: Elek Books.

Easton, D. 1959. "Political Anthropology," in *Biennial Review of Anthropology,* ed. by B. Siegel. Stanford, Calif.: Stanford University Press.

Eisenstadt, S. N. 1959. "Primitive Political Systems," *American Anthropologist,* LXI: 200–220.

———. 1963. *The Political System of Empires.* New York: The Free Press of Glencoe.

Evans-Pritchard, E. E. 1940. "The Political Organization of the Nandi-Speaking Peoples of Kenya," *Africa,* XIII: 250–67.

———. 1940b. *The Nuer.* London: Oxford University Press.

———. 1948. *Divine Kingship of the Shilluk of the Nilotic Sudan.* Cambridge: The University Press.

Fallers, L. A. 1956. *Bantu Bureaucracy.* Cambridge: W. Heffer and Sons.

———. 1959. "Despotism, Status Culture and Social Mobility," *Comparative Studies in Society and History,* II: 11–32.

———. 1963. "Political Sociology and the Anthropological Study of African Polities," *Archives européennes de sociologie,* IV: 311–29.

Fallers, M. C. 1960. *The Eastern Lacustrine Bantu.* Ethnographic Survey of Africa. London: International African Institute.

Foot, E. C. 1913. *A Galla-English, English-Galla Dictionary.* Cambridge: The University Press.

Fortes, M. 1960. "The Structure of Unilineal Descent Groups," in *Cultures and Societies of Africa,* ed. by S. and P. Ottenberg, 163–87. New York: Random House.

Fortes, M., and E. E. Evans-Pritchard, eds. 1940. *African Political Systems.* London: Oxford University Press.

Frankfort, H. 1948. *Kingship and the Gods.* Chicago: The University of Chicago Press.

Franzoj, A. 1885. *Continente Nero.* Turin: Roux and Favale.

Fried, M. H. 1960. "The Evolution of Social Stratification and the State," in *Culture in History,* ed. by S. Diamond. New York: Columbia University Press.

———. 1961. "Warfare, Military Organization, and the Evolution of Society," *Anthropologica,* n.s., III: 134–47.

Gluckman, M. 1940. "The Kingdom of the Zulu," in *African Political Systems,* ed. by M. Fortes and E. E. Evans-Pritchard. London: Oxford University Press.

———. 1951. "The Lozi of Barotseland," in *Seven Tribes of British Central Africa,* ed. by E. Colson and M. Gluckman. Manchester: Manchester University Press.

———. 1963. *Order and Rebellion in Tribal Africa.* London: Cohen and West.

Great Britain. 1922. *A Handbook of Abyssinia.* Great Britain: General Staff, War Office.

Greenberg, J. H. 1949. "The Negro Kingdoms of the Sudan," *Transactions of the New York Academy of Sciences,* ser. II, II: 126–35.

———. 1963. *The Languages of Africa.* Indiana University Research Center in Anthropology, Folklore, and Linguistics, Publication No. 25. Bloomington, Indiana.

Grühl, M. 1932. *The Citadel of Ethiopia.* London: Jonathan Cape.

———. 1938. *Zum Kaisergott von Kaffa.* Berlin: Schlieffer Verlag.

Guèbrè Sellassié. 1930–31. *Chronique du règne de Ménélik II.* ed. by M. de Coppet. 2 vols. Paris: Maisonneuve frères.

Guidi, I. 1907. "Storia dei loro regni (Meččа)," *Mitteilungen des Seminars für Orientalische Sprachen,* X: 15–18.

Gulliver, P., and P. H. Gulliver. 1953. *The Central Nilo-Hamites.* Ethnographic Survey of Africa. London: International African Institute.

Gulliver, P. H. 1958. "East African Age-Group Systems." Conference Paper of the East African Institute for Social Research, Markerere College.

Haberland, E. 1963. *Galla Süd-Äthiopiens.* Stuttgart: W. Kohlhammer.

Harris, W. C. 1844. *The Highlands of Aethiopia.* 3 vols. London: Longman, Brown, Green, and Longmans.

Huntingford, G. W. B. 1953. *The Southern Nilo-Hamites.* Ethnographic Survey of Africa. London: International African Institute.

———. 1955. *The Galla of Ethiopia; The Kingdoms of Kafa and*

Janjero. Ethnographic Survey of Africa. London: International African Institute.

Irstam, T. 1944. *The King of Ganda.* Stockholm: The Ethnographic Museum of Sweden. new ser., Publication No. 8.

Isenberg, C. W., and J. L. Krapf. 1843. *Journals of the Rev. Messrs. Isenberg and Krapf, Missionaries of the Church Missionary Society, Detailing their Proceedings in the Kingdom of Shoa, and Journeys in other Parts of Abyssinia, in the years 1839, 1840, 1841, and 1842.* London: Seeley, Burnside, and Seeley.

Kaberry, P. 1957. "Primitive States," *British Journal of Sociology,* VIII: 224–34.

Knutsson, K. E. 1963. "Social Structure of the Mecca Galla," *Ethnology,* II: 506–11

Kraeling, C. H., and R. M. Adams. 1960. *City Invincible.* Chicago: The University of Chicago Press.

Kuper, H. 1946. *An African Aristocracy.* London: Oxford University Press.

Levy, R. 1957. *The Social Structure of Islam.* Cambridge: The University Press.

Lewis, B. 1950. *The Arabs in History.* London: Hutchinson.

Lewis, H. S. 1962. "Historical Problems in Ethiopia and the Horn of Africa," *Annals of the New York Academy of Sciences,* XCVI: 504–11.

———. 1964. "A Reconsideration of the Socio-Political System of the Western Galla," *Journal of Semitic Studies,* IX: 139–43.

Lewis, I. M. 1959. "The Classification of African Political Systems," *Rhodes-Livingstone Journal,* XXV: 59–69.

Lienhardt, G. 1958. "The Western Dinka," in *Tribes Without Rulers,* ed. by J. Middleton and D. Tait. London: Routledge and Kegan Paul.

Lindblom, K. G. 1934. "Spears with Two or More Heads, Particularly in Africa," in *Essays Presented to C. G. Seligman.* London: Kegan Paul, Trench, and Trubner.

Lipsky, G. A. 1962. *Ethiopia: Its People, Its Society, Its Culture.* New Haven, Conn.: Human Relations Area Files Press.

Ludolphus, J. 1682. *A New History of Ethiopia.* London: Samuel Smith.

Mair, L. P. 1934. *An African People in the Twentieth Century.* London: G. Routledge and Sons.

———. 1962. *Primitive Government.* Baltimore, Md.: Penguin Books.

Massaja, G. 1885–95. *I Miei Trentacinque Anni di Missione nell'-Alta Etiopia.* 12 vols. Milan: Pontificia S. Guiseppe.

Meek, C. K. 1931. *A Sudanese Kingdom.* London: Kegan Paul, Trench, and Trubner.

Messing, S. D. 1957. "The Highland-Plateau Amhara of Ethiopia." Unpublished Ph.D. dissertation, University of Pennsylvania, Philadelphia.

Middleton, J., and D. Tait. 1958. *Tribes Without Rulers.* London: Routledge and Kegan Paul.

Montandon, G. 1913. *Au Pays Ghimirra.* Neuchatel: Attinger Frères.

Moreno, M. M. 1939. *Grammatica della Lingua Galla.* Milan: A. Mondadori.

———. 1940. *Manuale di Sidamo.* Milan: A. Mondadori.

Murdock, G. P. 1947. *Social Structure.* New York: The Mac-Millan Co.

———. 1959. *Africa: Its Peoples and Their Culture History.* New York: McGraw-Hill.

Nadel, S. F. 1942. *A Black Byzantium.* London: Oxford University Press.

Onneken, D. 1956. *"Die Königskultur Kaffas und der verwandten Königreiche."* Unpublished Ph.D. dissertation, Johann Wolfgang Goethe-Universität, Frankfurt am Main.

Pankhurst, R. 1961a. "Menelik and the Foundation of Addis Ababa," *Journal of African History,* II: 103–18.

———. 1961b. *An Introduction to the Economic History of Ethiopia.* London: Lalibela House.

Paulitschke, P. 1888. *Harar.* Leipzig: F. A. Brockhaus.

———. 1893–96. *Ethnographie Nordost-Afrikas.* 2 vols. Berlin: Geographische Verlagshandlung Dietrich Reimer.

Perham, M. 1948. *The Government of Ethiopia.* London: Oxford University Press.

Peristiany, J. G. 1939. *The Social Institutions of the Kipsigis.* London: G. Routledge and Sons.

Plowden, W. C. 1868. *Travels in Abyssinia and the Galla Country.* London: Longmans Green.

Polanyi, K., C. M. Arensberg, and H. Pearson, eds. 1957. *Trade and Markets in the Early Empires.* Glencoe, Ill.: The Free Press.

Prins, A. H. J. 1953. *East African Age-Class Systems.* Djakarta: J. B. Wolters.

Rattray, R. S. 1929. *Ashanti Law and Constitution.* London: Oxford University Press.

Richards, A. I. 1940. "The Political System of the Bemba Tribe," in *African Political Systems,* ed. by M. Fortes and E. E. Evans-Pritchard. London: Oxford University Press.

———, ed. 1960. *East African Chiefs.* New York: Frederick A. Praeger.

———. 1961. "African Kings and Their Royal Relatives," *Journal of the Royal Anthropological Institute,* XCI: 135–50.

Sadler, A. W. 1958. "An Interpretive Inventory of Max Weber's Categories for the Study of Religion and Society." Unpublished Ph.D. dissertation, Columbia University, New York.

Salviac, M. de. 1901. *Les Galla.* Paris: H. Oudin.

Schapera, I. 1956. *Government and Politics in Tribal Societies.* London: Watts.

Simoons, F. J. 1960. *Northwest Ethiopia.* Madison, Wis.: The University of Wisconsin Press.

Smith, M. G. 1956. "On Segmentary Lineage Systems," *Journal of the Royal Anthropological Institute,* LXXXVI: 39–80.

———. 1960. *Government in Zazzau.* London: Oxford University Press.

Soleillet, P. 1886. *Voyages en Ethiopie.* Rouen: Espérance Cagniard.

Southall, A. 1956. *Alur Society.* Cambridge: W. Heffer and Sons.

Southwold, M. n.d. *Bureaucracy and Chiefship in Buganda.* East African Studies, No. 14. Kampala, Uganda: East African Institute of Social Research.

Stenton, D. M. 1951. *English Society in the Early Middle Ages.* London: Penguin.

Stephenson, C. 1942. *Mediaeval Feudalism.* Ithaca, N.Y.: Cornell University Press.

Tordoff, W. 1962. "The Ashanti Confederacy," *Journal of African History,* III: 399–417.

Traversi, L. 1888. "Escursione nel Gimma," *Bollettino della Società Geografica Italiana,* XIII: 901–23.

Trimingham, J. S. 1952. *Islam in Ethiopia.* London: Oxford University Press.

Ullendorff, E. 1960. *The Ethiopians.* London: Oxford University Press.

Vansina, J. 1962. "A Comparison of African Kingdoms," *Africa,* XXXII: 324–35.

Viterbo, E. 1936. *Vocabolario della Lingua Oromonica.* Milan: U. Hoepli.

Von Grunebaum, G. E. 1954. *Medieval Islam.* Chicago: The University of Chicago Press.

———. 1955. *Islam: Essays in the Nature and Growth of a Cul-*

tural Tradition. The American Anthropological Association, Memoir No. 81.

Weber, M. 1947. *The Theory of Social and Economic Organization, trans.* by A. R. Henderson and T. Parsons. Glencoe, Ill.: The Free Press.

———. 1948. *From Max Weber: Essays in Sociology,* trans. by H. Gerth and C. W. Mills. London: Routledge and Kegan Paul.

———. 1962. *The City,* trans. by D. Martindale and G. Neuwirth. New York: Collier Books.

Wellby, M. S. 1901. *'Twixt Sirdar and Menelik.* New York: Harper and Brothers.

Winans, E. V. 1962. *Shambala: The Constitution of a Traditional State.* London: Routledge and Kegan Paul.

Wittfogel, K. 1957. *Oriental Despotism: A Comparative Study of Total Power.* New Haven: Yale University Press.

Wrigley, C. C. 1959. "The Christian Revolution in Buganda," *Comparative Studies in Society and History,* II: 33–48.

Zeitlin, M. 1960. "Max Weber on the Sociology of the Feudal Order," *The Sociological Review,* VIII: 203–7.

Index